George Blagden Bacon

The Sabbath Question

Sermons preached to the Valley Church, Orange, N. J.

George Blagden Bacon

The Sabbath Question
Sermons preached to the Valley Church, Orange, N. J.

ISBN/EAN: 9783337088040

Printed in Europe, USA, Canada, Australia, Japan

Cover: Foto ©Lupo / pixelio.de

More available books at **www.hansebooks.com**

The Sabbath Question

Sunday Observance and Sunday Laws

A SERMON AND TWO SPEECHES

BY

LEONARD WOOLSEY BACON

PASTOR OF THE PARK CHURCH, NORWICH, CONN.

Six Sermons on the Sabbath Question

BY THE LATE

GEORGE BLAGDEN BACON

PASTOR OF THE VALLEY CHURCH, ORANGE, N.J.

NEW YORK

G. P. PUTNAM'S SONS

27 AND 29 WEST 23D STREET

1882

PREFACE.

IT would not be presumptuous in me to infer from the diligence and ingenuity that have been used in publicly misrepresenting my position and course on the Sunday question, that the public have some interest in the matter. The object of this book, however, is, not to define my position, but to discuss the question,—a question in which the gravest interests are imperilled by untenable assumptions and arguments on both sides.

As to the misrepresentations that have been made, it is impossible to harbor serious resentment; for they seem to have been devoid of malice. Great consideration is due toward that unhappy class of our fellow-citizens who have become bound, under inhuman and demoralizing contracts, to be funny once in every twenty-four hours, honestly if they can, but — to be funny. Morality cannot always approve the expedients to which they think themselves compelled to resort in the distressing exigencies of their toilsome business; but, even where morality condemns, humanity may pity and forgive.

The best part of this book is made up of the "Six Sermons" of my noble and saintly brother

George, whose opinions, in the main, I accept as my own. If critical readers of the book shall be charmed with the clear spiritual insight, the lucid argument, and the faultless beauty of expression which mark these, like all he ever wrote, and shall find what I have written to be rude and little worth in the comparison, I shall be better pleased than with any commendation they could pronounce upon me. I hope the republication of these "Six Sermons" will draw wider attention to the forthcoming memorial of his life and writings, of which we all, father and brothers, regret the long delay.

POSTSCRIPT.

Since the copy of this book was prepared for the press, two events have occurred to hinder the publication of it: first, the stereotype plates of the "Six Sermons" were found to have been destroyed; and then, when arrangements to restore them had been completed, the sudden and serene departure of my father from the midst of his great labors for the kingdom of God on earth into the fulness of that "Sabbath-rest that remaineth for the people of God," interrupted the course of this business with its sorrow and its inexpressible joy and triumph.

LEONARD WOOLSEY BACON.

Norwich, Conn., Feb. 22, 1882.

CONTENTS.

	PAGE
PREFACE	3

I.

A SERMON AND TWO SPEECHES.

BY LEONARD WOOLSEY BACON.

1. PERSONAL DUTY REGARDING THE OBSERVANCE OF THE LORD'S DAY. Sermon to the Park Church, Norwich, Conn., September, 1879 9

2. SUNDAY LEGISLATION. Address at the Massachusetts Sabbath Conventions, Boston and Springfield, October, 1879 34
   NOTE. Letter addressed to the Judiciary Committee of the Legislature of Connecticut . . . 54

3. ENFORCEMENT OF SUNDAY LAWS. Speech to the Citizens of Norwich, Monday evening, Aug. 11, 1879, just after the public defiance of the Law of Connecticut for securing a weekly Day of Rest . . . 59

II.

SIX SERMONS ON THE SABBATH QUESTION.

BY GEORGE BLAGDEN BACON.

              PAGE

PREFACE 101

1. THE SABBATH OF GOD. Preached Feb. 23, 1868 . 105

2. THE PURPOSE OF THE JEWISH SABBATH. Preached March 1, 1868 124

3. THE USE AND ABUSE OF THE JEWISH SABBATH. Preached March 8, 1868 147

4. THE LORD'S DAY A PRIVILEGE. Preached March 22, 1868 173

5. THE LORD'S DAY HONORABLE. Preached March 29, 1868 204

6. THE RIGHT OBSERVANCE OF THE LORD'S DAY. Preached April 5, 1868 231

SUNDAY OBSERVANCE AND SUNDAY LAWS.

PERSONAL DUTY CONCERNING SUNDAY OBSERVANCE.

SERMON TO THE PARK CHURCH, NORWICH, SEPTEMBER, 1879.

"Let every man be fully persuaded in his own mind."
Rom. xiv. 5.

THE question, What is a Christian man's duty concerning the observance of the Lord's Day? is just now in the worst position into which a question of personal duty can possibly fall. It is in a position of vagueness and doubt. Men are not fully persuaded in their own minds about it, one way or the other. Consequently they are continually in the way of being tempted to do that which they suspect, or half suspect, to be wrong, or that which they are not quite sure to be right. When so tempted, most men yield to the temptation;

and, so yielding, they wound their own consciences and condemn their own souls. The conscience of the Christian Church amongst us is becoming miserably demoralized and broken down by this condition of things; and nothing can bring it back to a healthy tone, except a thorough clearing up of the intellect on the subject.

I do this generation no injustice in saying that the notions of duty on this subject that are current in Christian circles are not founded on intelligent, conscientious, personal study of the will of God concerning it. The opinions of our fathers, whether they were right or wrong, were so founded; and they held them clearly and firmly, and honored them by consistent practice. They were fully persuaded in their own minds. And we are persuaded in their minds, and not in our own. We have accepted their conclusions in a matter-of-course way, as a sort of tradition of the elders, taking .for granted that it must be right; and, when we are suddenly confronted with a different view, we are first a little shocked, and then a little shaken in mind, and then, some of us, a little censorious upon the wickedness of people that do not come up to our standard, and a little self-satisfied and vainglorious over our superior virtue; and, the rest of us, a little disposed to relax somewhat in our practice, with a feeling that we are not quite certain that it is wrong, or, if wrong, not certain that it is so *very* wrong. It is a wretched condition of the conscience and life, growing out of a poor, low condition of the intellect, which is vague and hazy and fluctuating on one of those questions of personal duty on which every man ought to be fully persuaded in his own mind.

One consequence of this traditionary way of dealing with the question of duty — this taking the law from one another, instead of taking it directly from the word of God — is, that "the good and acceptable and perfect will of God" becomes encumbered, as it was in the days of the Pharisees, by a system of conventionalities, written or unwritten, underneath which the law of God is quite lost out of sight. And naturally enough, when we come to comparing these conventional standards, the most rigorous will seem to be the most virtuous; so that by and by the rule of duty generally professed will be some impossible code of ascetic requirements, like that in the Westminster Catechism,[1] which demands that the whole day be devoted to unintermitted acts of spiritual meditation and religious worship, and condemns every word and thought that departs from spiritual topics, as a sin. A most disastrous thing, in the long run, is this refinement and improvement on the law of God. Some high and worthy souls will try to discipline themselves to such sustained spiritual flights, and with many a helpless fall, and many an hour of anxiety and self-reproach, will strive more and more for the attainment of that ideal, and with some measure of success. Others, holding still to the same rule of duty, give up the thought of conforming their conduct to it, and subject their whole lives to the shame and bondage of a willing, conscious, habitual short-coming.

---

[1] "The Sabbath is to be sanctified by a holy resting all that day, even from such worldly employments and recreations as are lawful on other days, and spending the whole time in the public and private exercises of God's worship, except so much as is to be taken up in the works of necessity and mercy."

Others, still, consider that, however doubtful they may be themselves about the traditionary rules of Sabbath observance, and however little they may conform to them in private, nevertheless the traditionary ideas on this subject are very salutary, and it is best to keep them up, as far as may be, by an outward show or sham of conformity. And, finally, there are others, and they are pitifully many, who find the regulations so imposed irksome, not to say impossible, and in violent and wicked rebellion cast off all cords of restraint, and declare that they don't care for God's law, and that they will do their own pleasure, whether God be for them or against them. Oh, there is a dreadful account of human sin, both open and hypocritical, both in the days of the Pharisees and in our own days, to be imputed to the setting up of a system of conventionalities, instead of the law of God, in the matter of the observance of the day of rest!

Now, instead of attempting to maintain and enforce the Sabbath of New England tradition, or the Sabbath of the Presbyterian Catechism, by culling "proof-texts" in support of them, I propose to go behind all traditions and prepossessions, and study the matter direct from the Holy Scriptures themselves.

1. The first thing, the last thing, the one thing, in all the Scriptures most conspicuous concerning the Sabbath day,—so conspicuous that almost every thing else concerning it is unimportant in the comparison,—is, that it is to be a day of rest. This is the meaning of the word Sabbath-day,—it means the rest-day. On the seventh day—the seventh cycle or creative period—God rested, and blessed (consecrated) the seventh day of every week for human rest from human toil. This is the main, primary object and ordinance of the day; and in all the law and the prophets there is no other ordinance distinctly given regarding it. Every one—high and low, householder and servant, even the very cattle, every one—is to knock off work, and rest. So it says in Genesis. So it says again in Exodus, and in Numbers, and over again in Deuteronomy, and yet again in Nehemiah, and in many

of the prophets. This was the public law of the land, as well as the law of each man's conscience before God. And it was enforced too. One Sabbath morning, while the people were still under martial law in the desert encampment, a man openly undertook to defy the law, and to make issue with the government on this point of obedience to the law of the weekly rest. His challenge to the government was accepted on the spot, and he was executed as if for treason to the law. And this was right. If punishment is ever right for any thing, it is right in its uttermost severity in the case of one who openly defies the law and the government, even if it is on a matter of gathering sticks, or a matter of firing balls at a bit of bunting. And the government that cannot, or dare not, or will not, deal with the open defiance of its authority, is a decaying and dying government; and such a government was not that of the Hebrew wanderers in the wilderness. When the law said, there shall be no work, but general rest, throughout the camp, the law meant what it said.

It meant what it said. That is really (if I

may tell you one of the secrets of theological science), that is really the key to the mysteries of biblical interpretation, — that the Bible means what it says. Now, in regard to this fourth commandment, there is a strong impression that in some mysterious way it means something that it does not say. What it says is so simple, — that on the seventh day they shall knock off work, and rest, — surely it cannot mean so simple a thing as that! There is, I suspect, an impression on some minds, that, if they could get at the original Hebrew, they could extort more of a meaning out of it than that, — that men were just to knock off work, and rest. But I think the Hebrew is as plain as the English.

But is not more than this meant when it is commanded to "sanctify" the Sabbath day, or "keep it holy"? I think not, and I will tell you why. First, as I judge, the meaning of the opening words of the commandment are to be interpreted by the words that follow; and, thus interpreted, they mean that the day is to be kept sacred from the intrusion of labor. Secondly, the meaning of these words is to be judged from the whole course of divine instruction and requirement concerning the Sabbath day; and that is directed simply and exclusively to this one point of abstinence from labor. Thirdly, it is to be judged by common sense; and this excludes the idea, that to keep the Sabbath holy was to "spend all the time in worship:" for no ordinary mind, not one in a hundred, — not one in a hundred thousand, — is capable of sustained acts of worship twenty-four hours, or twelve hours, or six hours, in continuance; and this commandment was not given to extraordinary minds, such as go to make up a Westminster Assembly of theologians, but to mankind at large, and primarily to a very unspiritual part of mankind, — to a clan of freedmen just come forth from the house of bondage.

"But is that all that the commandment requires?" The question is put sometimes in that spirit of Naaman the Syrian, which cannot believe that God would command a simple, easy, happy thing, — a spirit which has misconstrued God's word on more vital matters than this matter of the rest-day. "Is that all?"

Well, is not that enough to begin on? Had you not better wait till you have learned to fulfil this plain and easy injunction, before you go on to look for some more recondite and weighty meaning? Do you fulfil it? There is no scandal about your deportment. You would be offended and pained to see your neighbor, whose daily work is done with a spade or a grocer's wagon, going about it of a Sunday morning. But your work is done with your head: and when you carry your six days' work over into the seventh, and instead of taking the happy repose which is your privilege and duty, and your privilege because it is your duty, you are busy, in your place in church, or as you sit with the religious newspaper on your lap, maturing business combinations, getting a complicated bargain into the right shape, calculating a new turn in politics, or threading the intricacies of a lawsuit, and all this without any visible sign of it on your countenance, — why, there is no one to be disturbed or scandalized by it; but it is in distinct, diametric disagreement with this commandment, both in its letter and in its spirit, — far more clearly so than if you were to take your hoe into your flower-garden, or drag your lawn-mower across the turf; for these are not your work, but your recreation. Every thing is done with perfect decorum and stillness, when you take your hard six days' head-work over into the seventh; but it does not the less suffer the retributions which, in the course of nature, overtake the violations of a commandment that is contained not less in the principles of physiology than in the beneficent written law.

But is not the Sabbath ordained for worship? No, not primarily; but for repose and refreshment. Only once in the multitude of commands concerning the Sabbath day, is mention made of "a holy convocation:"[1] the Hebrew ritual also made some distinction between the seventh-day ceremonies and those of other days.[2] But the law and meaning of the day are given in the fourth commandment in its two varying forms,[3] and they are perfectly clear. Nevertheless, worship and the study of God's will did grow to be a beautiful and con-

---

[1] Lev. xxiii. 2, 3. [2] Num. xxviii. 9; Lev. xxiv. 8.
[3] Exod. xx. 8-11; Deut. v. 12-15.

stant incident of the day of rest. As the scenes of public history move swiftly by us in the early books of the Old Testament, we get here and there a glimpse of domestic life, and among these the picture of a godly family saddling its beasts to go to the prophet's house.[1] Once or twice in the Psalms [2] we seem to hear a burst of Sabbath worship; and at last, after the return from exile, we find the synagogue, the type of the Christian church, wherein "Moses is preached every Sabbath day,"[3] grown into universal acceptance. And all this, not by ordinance, but all the more to the honor of God and his church because it is without ordinance — the native growth of a willing worship upon a divinely given rest-day.

2. Such was the use of the Sabbatic law under the Old Testament. What were the abuses and perversions of it, the pages of the Four Gospels repeatedly show. That spirit to which I have already alluded as infecting, not Jewish only, but Christian interpretations of

---

[1] 2 Kings iv. 22.   [2] Psa. lxxxi. 3; xcii. title.
[3] Acts xv. 21.   Cf. Acts xiii. 14, 15, 27; Luke iv. 15, 16.

Scripture, could not be content with the plain and simple thing which the Scripture said, but must needs superinduce upon it new meanings by construction and inference; thus devising new prohibitions, and thereby inventing new temptations and new sins,—a most perilous and pernicious business. "Carrying a bed!" said they, when they saw one that had been sick of the palsy. "Nay, verily; that is transportation. If a bed, why not all your household furniture? Where can you draw the line? Rubbing out corn in the hands! what is that but a form of threshing? and killing a flea is tantamount to hunting. And if one were to climb a tree, and thereby break a twig of it, he might as well have chopped wood all day." Of course, under this sort of interpretation, the suffering or imposing of the worst annoyances was a mark of the highest virtue. The ascetic treatment of the day transformed it from a privilege into a slavish burden. There was no point on which Pharisaism so bitterly attacked the conduct of Jesus; none on which his protest against the Pharisees, as making void the law which they pretended to guard, was more pointed. His contention against them was, not that the Mosaic Sabbath was an intolerable burden, but that the intolerable burden which they bound on men's shoulders was not the Mosaic Sabbath, but a travesty of it. These artificial austerities, not only were they not required, they were forbidden by the whole genius of the day.

Thus the clear meaning of the ancient law is confirmed by the authority of Jesus Christ in his rebuke of current misinterpretations. The object of the Sabbath law was plain enough. Other blessings were incidental to it. A whole system of useful religious observances had grown up around it. But the primary object of the institution was *rest*,— that each one should rest himself, and allow all others to rest. This was the law. Christ did not attempt to modify it. He restored it wherein it had been made void by misinterpretation. The Sabbath, he said, was not an end, but a means to an end. The Sabbath law was a law of universal rest; but it was enacted for the benefit of mankind, and is therefore to be held subordinate to human wants and necessities. In short, he laid down the principle that is incorporated into our own legislation on the day of rest, — that suspension of labor is not to be exacted in case of works of necessity or mercy. But he did not change the character of the Hebrew festival, or add any new commandment to that which made it a day of personal and public repose. The ordinance that "all the time be spent in acts of public or private worship" is not found in the Old Testament or in the New, but in the acts of the Westminster Assembly of Divines. It does not appear that he whom, alone of men, we call our Lord, spent his Sabbaths in that way. In fact, the contrary appears at that dinner-party of a chief Pharisee, at which he was a conspicuous guest.

But now let us come closer to the personal, practical question which concerns and sometimes perplexes you and me. The question is, not what was the duty of a faithful Hebrew respecting the seventh day of the week, but what is the duty of an American Christian concerning the first day. And that, let us plainly acknowledge, is not to be defined by the letter of the law of Moses. We are not under the law, but under grace. We do not pretend to follow the letter of the fourth commandment. We have even conspicuously and quite unnecessarily departed from the letter of it at a point on which the commandment insists with great emphasis, alleging it as containing the very reason of the commandment. The commandment says, Keep the seventh day sacred to repose, because on the seventh day the Lord your God rested from the labors of the creation. We say, No: we will keep the first day of the week for other reasons. And when the Seventh Day Baptists reproach us with this unfaithfulness to the law which we profess so punctiliously to observe, we have really very little to say for ourselves; and so we generally turn them off with some poor little joke: for the most of an argument that I remember to have heard against the Seventh Day Baptists, was the one which used to be rehearsed once a year by the Professor of Astronomy at Yale College, when, at a certain point in his lectures, he advised them all to sail around the world to the eastward, and so gain a day in their reckoning, and they would come back all right, and quite like other people. The day doesn't matter (we say with a fine and lofty contempt), so long as it is one day in seven. The day does matter, says the fourth commandment; and it shall be the seventh day, for such and such a reason. The day does matter, said the early Christians; and we decide, not to keep the seventh day, but the first, for such and such another reason. The very ground of the change was, that it did make a difference which day was observed, and that the difference was worth making. And it has this noble instruction for us, if only we have ears and hearts to receive it, that the laws of commandments contained in ordinances — the formulas, "touch not, taste not, handle not, which perish in the using" — are not a sufficient measure and gauge of the Christian's duty. Every Lord's Day that we gather for worship in the midst of the general calm and silence of a public rest is a declaration at the same time of our loyalty to the spirit of the law, and of our freedom from its letter. It is a sign that we have taken, not a lower and laxer standard of duty, but a higher, — the law interpreted by the spirit of grateful love.

Applying, now, this standard to the practical and personal questions of duty touching the Lord's Day, we find that:—

I. Some of these questions may be eliminated at once, as being settled by other considerations.

1. Many questions on which we ask for light from the fourth commandment are fully decided for us under the fifth, by the law of the household of which we are members, by the known wish of the father and mother whom we honor and obey.

2. Other questions may be settled for us in like manner by the civil law to which we owe allegiance, and which limits us in our liberty of deciding and acting at certain points.

3. Duty to the church — the community of the fellow-Christians among whom we live — may often be a consideration that shall justly decide questions of duty concerning the day of

rest, quite independently of their intrinsic merits. The fact that this line of argument is so often exaggerated and overstrained in our time must not lead us to forget that it is a legitimate and authoritative line of argument.

II. But setting aside all such questions, thankful to be relieved of them, there will still keep coming back to us questions of Lord's Day observance to be decided squarely and directly. What can I say that shall be helpful to you to reach a right conclusion on them?

I cannot but think that my personal experience has prepared me in some degree to advise upon this subject; for the question has been forced upon my decision in circumstances in which no one of these outside considerations could come in to make weight, — in countries where there was neither public sentiment, nor Christian feeling, nor civil law, nor filial duty, to help decide. I have always been glad, for myself and my family, that I was led to keep the same quiet, religious, and family Sunday in Germany and Switzerland that I had learned to keep here in New England. And however difficult, at times, it was, I believe still that it was the right thing, the incomparably best thing, for me and my children. I do not ask you to accept my rule. I invite no man to judge me concerning holy days, and I myself judge no man. Be persuaded each in your own mind. But ponder well the *principle* which I commend to you, the axiom which cannot be wrong, that in this, as in all things else, *you are bound before God to do the very best thing*, and nothing but the best.

I seem to hear the answer coming back with a sigh from burdened hearts, "It is only a new way of saying the old thing. To do the very best, and nothing but the best, what can this mean but to impose upon us the strain of twelve or fifteen hours of incessant religious exercises,—the yoke which neither we nor our fathers were able to bear?"

To which I have only to say, that, if it is true that this is the best, then you are bound to it. And if your relaxation of this rule means that you give up trying to do your best in God's service, and mean to do only your second-best, then are you condemned in that which you allow. But it is not true. The history of your individual conscience, as well as the history of society, proves that this exaggeration of the law of God is neither for his glory nor for the good of his human creatures. We must go behind this "tradition of the elders" for the true rule of a Christian man's duty on the Lord's Day.

1. We find it in the words of the ancient law, — the law of *rest*, — rest of body and mind. How strangely good people sometimes miss it! Often, passing Sunday away from home, I have heard my hosts confess, with half a blush, that they were guilty of having a late breakfast Sunday morning. And oftener still I have heard some of those bustling, stir-about Christians, whom we have all met with, claiming, with much complacency, that his Sunday was the hardest day of all the week to him, — that what with church-going, and Sunday schools, and prayer-meetings, and street-preaching, and all, he got up earlier, worked harder, and went to bed wearier, than any other day, — all which may be right, but it is not resting.

2. Do I need to say that it ought to be the

glory of the Lord's Day in a Christian family that it is the home-day? This is one of the pleasant things in the remembrance of our Sundays abroad, — the great processions of the baby-wagons on every public promenade and pleasant country-road. There were sights and sounds of demoralizing carousal on the one hand, and of enforced drudgery on the other hand; but the pleasant family groups about the baby-wagons were among the good things left to them of a day of rest.

It does seem as if sometimes amongst us a false notion of the sanctity of the day was suffered to hinder our sanctifying it by holy uses of family duty and affection. If ever old age, or sickness, or pining loneliness, are suffered to lack the enlivening of your visit, because you hold the day too holy for Sunday calls, the wrong is almost identical with that of those whom our Lord rebuked, who would say to their parents, "*Corban* — it is consecrated to holy uses — that which should have gone to your comfort and support."[1]

3. Let a systematic part of your Sabbath

---

[1] Mark vii. 11; Matt. xv. 5.

service be the doing of *works of mercy*. "Pure religious worship, and undefiled before God and the Father is this: To visit the fatherless and widow in their affliction, and to keep yourselves unspotted from the world." Pre-eminently is the Lord's Day the day for the deacons and deaconesses of the church to be busy on their official errands to the poor.

4. Finally, among the duties of the Christian Sabbath are public worship and instruction. I name them last, because, to those who spend the day in the spirit of these suggestions, there will be no need of enjoining them at all as a duty. They will come of themselves. They were not named in the original law of the Sabbath, but see how naturally and universally they came to be used; so that in Paul's day, as in ours, wherever there were Jews, there was a synagogue, and in it preaching and worship every Sabbath day.[1] If you keep this day to the Lord as a day of rest, of home comfort, of good works to the poor and the sick, I have no concern at all but that you will use it, in due proportion, for direct acts

[1] Acts xv. 21.

of worship. And the worship that you render will not be the less acceptable to the heart of God, the incense of your pure offering will not be of a less sweet savor, being the willing sacrifice of a thankful heart, than if, under the imagined stress of law, you were putting the mind on a continual and conscious strain to spend "all the time either in public or private worship."

The common mistake, in this whole business, is the mistake of supposing that the Lord's Day is so much time that the Lord has taken away from you that he might reserve it for himself. Nay, on the contrary, he has claimed it for himself that he might give it back to you. Once a week he comes between you and your employers, between you and your exacting business, your perplexities, your anxieties. It is to these that he turns in your behalf, and says, "Stand off a while. Let that man alone. Let him rest. This is my day."

And then he turns to you, and says, "This is my day, — the Sabbath of the Lord thy God. I have redeemed it, and guarded it, that I might give it back to thee. It was made for man. The Son of man is Lord of the Sabbath day. The Lord's Day is thine own day — thine."

And now, what will you do with it, — this free day, God's free gift to you? Will you toss it back into the midst of this world's cares and toils, to be ravened up by them? Will you consume it greedily in selfish pleasures, reckless of others' burdens of toil, that you may riot? Will you make of it "a day to afflict the soul, and bow down the head like a bulrush?" It were like flinging back the gift into the giver's face. Or will you rather rest in the Lord with a thankful and peaceful heart, so resting that others may have rest as well as you? Will you make the Sabbath a delight in your home? Will you be abundant in Christ-like acts of mercy, and "joyful in the house of prayer?"

SUNDAY LEGISLATION:

A LAW OF REST FOR ALL NECESSARY TO THE LIBERTY OF REST FOR EACH.

ADDRESS AT THE MASSACHUSETTS SABBATH CONVENTIONS, BOSTON AND SPRINGFIELD, OCTOBER, 1879.

MR. CHAIRMAN AND FELLOW-CITIZENS, — I purpose scrupulously to refrain from overstepping the narrow limits of the thesis on which I have been asked to speak, in any such way as to encroach on ground occupied by others. But there is one point essential to a right understanding of this and of many other parts of the subject before us, which, through the regretted absence of Judge Strong, has failed to be formally set before the convention,[1] and which, therefore, I may be permitted to illustrate by an incident that

---

[1] Judge Strong of the Supreme Court of the United States had been expected to read a paper on "The Civil and the Religious Sabbath."

occurred in the first International Sabbath Congress, held three years ago at Geneva.

After many hours of conference and discussion, the Congress had been brought to the point of adopting the platform of a permanent international Sabbath league; and of this platform a conspicuous article was the one embodying a "scriptural basis" (as it was called) consisting of the fourth commandment and the declaration of our Saviour, "The Sabbath was made for man." The question being on the adoption of this article, a fair-haired, near-sighted, and broad-shouldered gentleman, who had been thus far an earnest and useful member of the convention, arose, and very modestly and courteously asked (in the German language) that no basis of organization should be insisted on which would exclude him and those whom he represented from co-operation in a work so beneficent as the maintenance of a weekly day of rest. He himself was a rationalist pastor from Bremen: he was the representative of an "Arbeiterverein," or some sort of workingmen's organization of a socialist complexion; and neither he nor the Bremen workingmen had any kind of faith in the "scriptural basis," in Old Testament or New, which was proposed as a condition of co-operation. Only they felt that a weekly day of rest, guarded and guaranteed by law, would be an immense blessing to the workingman and to the whole public; and they asked the privilege of doing what they could, in their own way, and acting from their own point of view, in co-operation with those who differed from them in opinion, to promote the end which they all sought in common.

With many expressions of personal respect, the Congress nevertheless voted by an overwhelming majority to allow their unorthodox brother no part nor lot with them in their efforts to promote a social and legislative reform. But I have the satisfaction of assuring you that this action was not taken without an energetic remonstrance from the representative of the United States, who objected to hearing America cited as an example of enforcing religious duties by secular laws, and declared that our American Sunday legislation, which they so admired, was founded, not on the principle of enforcing a religious duty by civil law, but on the democratic principles of liberty, equality, and fraternity, — principles which we believe that we understand quite as well in America as they do in Geneva or Paris. A religious basis, he declared, was considered in America to be essential to co-operation in religious movements; but that we did not always find it necessary to quote scripture in a political manifesto, though this was sometimes done. It was important, he said, that those who undertook to deal with the Sabbath question should remember that the Sabbath question is not one question, but two questions; that the religious Sabbath, consecrated to worship and to divine commemoration, and the civil holiday, maintained by force of law, have this in common, that in many countries they coincide upon the same day; but they are not the same: the former cannot be enforced by secular legislation; and the latter cannot in this age be sustained merely by Bible-texts.

It was not much of a speech, but it made something of an impression; and the speaker was entirely contented with the result of it, when, in the great closing assembly, the most eloquent *conférencier* in the French language, Ernest Naville, took this distinction for his text, and, in a discourse of more than an hour's duration, commended the religious Sabbath to the observance of every good Christian, and the civil Sabbath to the support of every right-minded citizen, Christian or not. I wish this exquisitely lucid address might be added, in English, to our scanty stock of good popular literature relating to the subject. It might help to supersede some of the superstitious and fanatical literature now or lately current, from the effects of which the Sabbath cause is suffering.

Let me ask you, in order to avoid the misunderstanding which will otherwise be inevitable, to keep this distinction in mind, and remember that, throughout this paper, I am speaking primarily, not of the religious, but of the civil institution.

I shall presume, then, on your good sense and clear apprehension in this matter, taking for granted that you are wiser than the narrowness of the International Congress, and that, on the enforcement of the external quiet and repose of the civil Sunday (which I understand to be the aspect of the question on which I am invited to speak), you are willing to entertain a line of argument broad and liberal enough to demand the adhesion and support of every reasonable man, whatever his views concerning the religious sanctions of the day.

The question is one of — what shall I say? workingmen's rights, I was about to say, except that this expression has become so smutted in the dirty hands of demagogues, that one loathes to take it up after them, — the question is one of personal liberty; how to secure for every citizen the liberty to rest one day in seven.

There is a very free and easy answer to this question on the tongue's end of some wise people, who deliver it as an axiom that the short and ready way to universal liberty of resting is simply to keep hands off, not to meddle with the matter by legislation, and let everybody do as he pleases about it. What can be simpler?

The temptation is irresistible, to answer

these people according to their folly, and condemn them out of their own mouths. For it happens, curiously enough, that many of the very people who are clamoring against our *six-day law*, as an unwarrantable interference with individual liberty, are just as clamorous in favor of an *eight-hour law* of their own invention. "What do you want," let me ask, "of an eight-hour law? Why not leave the matter to every man to decide for himself, whether he shall work eight hours, or ten, or fifteen? Don't let us have any meddlesome legislation. 'The best government is that which governs least.' Surely, if your reasoning is good concerning days in the week, it is equally good concerning hours in the day!"

This argument has been curiously and admirably anticipated in the speech of Macaulay in defence of the principle of a ten-hour law, in the House of Commons, in 1846. The right and expediency of guarding the liberty to rest, by legally limiting the time of labor, was vindicated against this very objection by the analogy of the Sunday laws. Objectors said, "If this ten-hour limitation be good for the working-people, rely on it that they will themselves establish it without any law." — "Why not reason," answered Macaulay, — "why not reason in the same way about the Sunday? Why not say, 'If it be a good thing for the people of London to shut their shops one day in seven, they will find it out, and will shut their shops without a law?' Sir, the answer is obvious. I have no doubt, that, if you were to poll the shop-keepers of London, you would find an immense majority, probably a hundred to one, in favor of closing shops on the Sunday: and yet it is absolutely necessary to give to the wish of the majority the sanction of a law; for, if there were no such law, the minority, by opening their shops, would soon force the majority to do the same."[1]

How curiously the wheel of this discussion has come around, so that now there is a party of people soberly alleging what that famous orator enunciated as an absurdity, and claiming as an axiom what he proved from the premises which they are trying to knock away!

[1] Speeches of Macaulay, ed. Tauchnitz, ii. 208, 209. The whole speech is worth reading for its close relation to our subject.

This whole subject gets its liveliest illustration when, from time to time, some one of those vocations which the general convenience allows to be excepted from the general law of Sunday rest seeks to be included within the law. Repeatedly, for instance, there have been memorials from all the barbers of a town, asking to have their own shops shut by law. Very absurd, isn't it? If they want their shops shut, why don't they shut them? This was the view taken by one enterprising young colored man in a Connecticut town, not long ago. There was a movement, among his competitors in the profession, to have all the barbers' shops shut on Sunday. "All right!" he said, "you go right on, and shut your shops. Never mind me." And so all the shops had to be kept open.

Another illustration of a like character comes to me from a similar quarter. A coal-dealer, near a certain steamboat-landing, finds that in the competitions of business his Sunday rest has been completely taken away from him. All the little tugs and propellers find that they can get their coal put in on Sunday, and so they come Sunday in preference to any other day. Says he, "I don't so much as get time to go to early mass, and I am compelled to keep busy from morning till night. I can't refuse them; for if I do they will quit me altogether, and I shall lose my business. *I wish to heaven that some one would prosecute me!*" A clearer illustration of the value of the law of rest for all, in securing the liberty of rest for each one, can hardly be asked for, than this case of a man who wants to be prosecuted himself in order to protect him from the necessity of doing what he does not want to do, but has to do because he is at liberty to do it.

I put it to the whole trade of labor-reformers, who want to begin their reforms by breaking down the best existing safeguard of the workingman's liberty of rest and leisure, — I put the question to them, and beg for an answer if there is one to be given. After you have succeeded — I do not say in amending or repealing, but in defying and nullifying, our *six-day law*, how much good is your eight-hour law likely to do you, supposing that you get it passed? You succeed, by mere defiant law-breaking, in trampling down a statute venerable with use, anchored deep in the traditions of the people, and consecrated by many a solemn religious sanction. And you propose to set up in place of it a novel invention of your own, called an "eight-hour law." Do you suppose, that, when you have taught the public how little you care for law when it interferes with your convenience, you will find it an easy matter to enforce law against others when it interferes with their convenience?

But here I wish, with perfect candor, to answer a question which does not seem to me to be adequately answered by the average "evangelical Christian" in his arguments on this subject. Our German friend will ask whether it is not possible to make a distinction between the prohibition of labor, and the prohibition of recreation and orderly and innocent amusement. And *my* answer to him is (whatever yours may be), "Yes, it is possible, though it may be difficult; and, whenever as orderly citizens you choose to move in this direction for amendments of the law, we are ready to discuss your proposals with simple reference to the greatest good of the greatest number." It is useless for us to say that public amusements, however quiet and orderly, involve labor on some one's part. So does public worship. It is labor to blow a church-organ, as much as to blow a concert-hall organ. No legislation pretends to protect *every one's* Sunday rest. The general principle is modified by considerations of public convenience and expediency. There is nothing in the world, then, to hinder us from entering into the candid discussion of any proposed amendment intended to relax the rigor of the law concerning amusements, while still guarding, as far as possible, the provisions of the law concerning labor. Some of you will object, perhaps, that, in our duties as citizens, we are bound to be governed by the divine teachings, and that legislation ought to be conformed to the word of God. Agreed. But then, nothing is so clearly revealed in the word of God, whether in Old Testament or in New, if men would but see it, as this, — that the divine rule of public legislation is the rule of expediency, and not the rule of absolute right and wrong. The divine example of public legislation is to give "laws that are not good," when such laws are, on the whole, the best that the case admits. Legislation is never more contrary to the word of God, than when it is rigorously conformed to the word of God, without regard to expediency, local and temporary. I repeat it, then: there is nothing in our convictions of religious duty to hinder us from candidly discussing any measure that may be considered to be for the good of society, and looking towards a relaxation of the Sunday law respecting amusements, while maintaining it in vigor respecting labor. Possibly this might be accomplished by carefully amending the law. But one thing is perfectly sure, *it can't be done by breaking the law.* You cannot break this statute half across, and leave the other half sound. Some of these fine days, as business grows brisk, you will get back from your Sunday excursion or beer-garden, and find a notice that next Sunday, owing to pressure of business, the factory will run, or the shop will be open, and that you are wanted for a day's work. And if you think that then you will be able to plead, for your rest and your liberty, the very statute that you have defiantly broken for your amusement, you will have ample time and opportunity to find out your mistake.

Here, after all, we face this subject in its gravest aspect. For I say it with all respect to this assembly, yet not expecting you to agree with me, — expecting, rather, that some of you will be shocked when you hear it said, — that the sanctity of the Sabbath is not so serious a matter as the sanctity of human law and government; that the damage and peril to society, the church, the state, and the affront to the authority of God, in the habitual public defiance of the Sunday laws, consist less in the violation of the commandment than they do in the violation of the statute. The divine authority less distinctly binds us to the commandment than it binds us to the statute. There are, amongst us, citizens of many different religions, and citizens of no religion at all; and, even among Christian citizens, there are the widest conscientious variations as to the binding force of the fourth commandment on the individual and the state; and still further variations as to the nature of the duties which that commandment enjoins, if it is binding. You may lament these variations; you may hold them blameworthy; but you cannot deny the fact that they exist; and it will have a very wholesome effect on our dealings with the matter, to look this inexorable fact distinctly in the face, and to bear habitually in mind, that the traditionary notions of sabbatical duty to which we are accustomed are the notions only of a very small party in the Christian church. But here is a point on which the divine will is unmistakable, — a point on which there is no room for variation among Christians, or among good citizens; to wit, that the laws of man are to be obeyed as under God's authority, and for God's sake. The peril of the present time is not half so much that we are becoming a nation of Sabbath-breakers, as that we are becoming — as a well-known writer has recently said — "a nation of law-breakers." [1] The question, whether the Sun-

---

[1] Dangerous Tendencies in American Society.

day laws shall be amended, or even repealed, and the common rest-day of rich and poor be left unprotected from the rapacity of commercial and industrial competition, is a question which, grave and portentous as it is, it is nevertheless possible to contemplate with equanimity. Whenever this question comes up, we are bound to meet our fellow-citizens with patient argument, and abide the arbitrament of the ballot-box. Under our form of government, if the majority, on such a point, will be fools, there is no way but to let them learn their folly by the consequences. But to this other question, whether law, while it is law, shall be enforced and obeyed, there is but one answer compatible with the dignity or life of the state.

The argument which I have now set forth approves the Sunday laws of any state only so far as those laws confine themselves, with simplicity and good faith: first, to maintaining the day of rest from labor as a universal privilege; and, secondly, to taking the necessary precautions lest the privilege be abused to the detriment of public order and morals. For any thing beyond this, these laws must find their defence — if there is any rational defence to be found — in some other line of reasoning. But there can be no higher act of wisdom on the part of those who desire to see the universal repose and quiet order of the New-England Sabbath day revived and perpetuated, than, of their own accord, to see to it that our Sunday laws are cleared of every thing which they ought not to contain. The early legislation of New England on this subject was undoubtedly directed, in some particulars, to the enforcement of a *religious* observance of the day. This was consistent with the State-Church, or rather the Church-State, notions of that time: it is utterly irreconcilable with our own principles. I do not know that any vestige of it remains. Judging from the digest of the Sunday laws of New England, lately published by my friend, Walter Learned,[1] our statute-books are clear of any remainder of it. If not, they ought to be.

Further, we are suffering, both in the community and in private consciences, the re-action

[1] In Good Company, No. 2.

from overstrained statements concerning sabbatical duty. There is a canon of Sunday observance, written, not in the scriptures of either Testament, but in the Westminster Catechism and the traditions of the elders, commanding that "the entire time" that can be spared from works of necessity or mercy shall be "spent in acts of worship, public or private." I do not speak of this as a rule that is seriously professed by any of us. On the contrary, we have, one and all, abandoned it as a rule of our own action; and we keep it, if at all, only for torturing tender consciences, and for judging our neighbors by. But it would not be altogether strange if the spirit of it might be found lurking here and there in some neglected corner of the statute-book. If so, it is of high importance to the success of our cause that it be exorcised.

Further still, it is not an unheard-of thing for earnest and zealous labors in behalf of a good cause to become infected with that other spirit, which has been alleged to have Boston for its metropolis, but which has its spheres of lively activity in many a place beside, — the spirit of "malignant philanthropy." It is this spirit that is slanderously imputed to the English Puritans, who interfered with bear-baiting, it is said, less out of pity to the bear than out of spite at the enjoyment of the bystanders. How naturally it attaches itself to such matters as we have in hand, might be illustrated by many instances; but it is enough to take a single one from Mr. Gilbert Hamerton. He tells us of a certain neighborhood in Scotland, along the shore of a loch which it was sometimes necessary to cross on Sunday. The local code of ethics permitted the crossing in such cases, but on condition that it should be made with a row-boat, not with a sail-boat. The row-boat involved, indeed, more labor; but the sail-boat might involve *enjoyment*, and this was a thing to be prevented at any sacrifice! If our Sunday laws are to be preserved and enforced, it must be made unmistakably plain that the object, both of the law and of its enforcement, is *not* to prevent enjoyment, but to secure the universal privilege of rest from labor without detriment to the good order and morals of society. No reasonable person will deny that it is competent for the same law which interferes to liberate men from labor, to interfere to protect society from the disorderly abuse of this liberty. The question of the manner and degree of either interference is an open question, to be decided by considerations of expediency.

We cannot, fellow-citizens, keep it too distinctly in mind that this part of the Sabbath question, the matter of Sunday laws, is a matter of government and police, — a political matter; and I know of no way of carrying political measures, in a republic, but to have votes enough. There is, indeed, a certain class of reformatory politicians who have a mystical idea of carrying elections without votes, — to whom there is no scripture in all the Bible so precious as that of the thinning-out of Gideon's army. These are men of faith, who believe that a few warm-hearted, earnest citizens, that will march fearlessly and vigorously up to the polls, and jam their tickets into the ballot-box with sufficient energy, can easily outvote ten times their number. It is well for us to leave this sort of imbecility to the school of professional reformers to whom it belongs, and coolly to take the measure of the difficulties of the situation, — for it has difficulties. The measures that are to be carried and enforced, let us remember, will not be carried by the votes exclusively of evangelical Christians of orthodox doctrinal views, — that is, not without a very extraordinary revival in the mean time. It is well that we should ask ourselves whose the other votes are to be. It is well, for every reason, that we should put ourselves on ground so solid, so broad, so unselfish and unpartisan, so clearly right, that no reasonable man can object to it as unreasonable; that we should refuse to allow this great social interest to be complicated with other questions; in short, that we should *narrow the issue,* and *widen the basis of co-operation.*

NOTE. — The following letter was addressed to the Judiciary Committee of the Connecticut Legislature, in support of the writer's memorial for a Commission of Inquiry concerning the Sunday Laws.

GENTLEMEN, — Until the latest moment, I have been in hopes of appearing before you to-morrow, in conformity with your invitation, to give the reasons for my petition for a commission of inquiry as to the need of an amendment of the Sunday laws of the State. I submit the more willingly to the urgent personal reasons which prevent my going to Hartford, because I hope that my written communication will accomplish all that is needful, with a saving of the time of the committee.

Suffer me, at the outset, to forestall a possible misconception. I do not seek or desire any enforcement of a religious observance of Sunday. The objects of Sunday legislation should be simply and solely these two: first, to secure, as nearly as possible, to every citizen the privilege of rest from labor; secondly, to provide that the general rest of the community shall not be abused to the detriment of good order and morals. If the law goes beyond this, with any needless interference with convenience, pleasure, or even amusement, it thereby tends to defeat its own permanent effectiveness; and the pretence which is clamorously made, year after year, that the law is thus excessive, is itself a reason, not indeed for hasty amendment, but for deliberate and careful inquiry, such as the petition asks for.

But the main reason for a commission of inquiry is that alleged in the petition; to wit, that the laws in question not only are openly and habitually violated, but in some cases, when the enforcement of them has been attempted, have been insolently defied and nullified. It is obvious that the successful defiance of the law by influential corporations does more than to retrench certain clauses that stand in the way of their convenience: it practically abrogates the statute, with its unspeakable blessings to the community; it inflicts a shameful insult on the State, and weakens that respect for the laws which all good citizens are bound to cherish. These are grave reasons, I do not say for legislation, but for inquiry.

The most flagrant and insolent violations of the law are Sunday steamboat excursions, in defence of which considerations of humanity and public good are sometimes urged with apparent seriousness. Such considerations may much better be urged in favor of amending the law, than of defying and nullifying the law.

And I submit to you, gentlemen, that the allegation of them is a sufficient reason for inquiry into the truth of them. A commission duly authorized might easily ascertain whether such excursions, as now conducted in violation of law, are really the occasions of harmless recreation and refreshment that they are claimed to be, or orgies of debauchery such as they are alleged sometimes to be; and might furnish to a future General Assembly materials for a wise judgment on the question, whether if they were made lawful, so that they might be conducted by law-abiding citizens instead of law-breakers, and vigilantly policed, instead of being exempted, as now, from all police supervision whatever, the change would be for the general advantage. The question is an open and legitimate one, and of grave importance.

To sum up, then: every argument that is used, either in crimination or in defence, is an argument in favor of legislative inquiry; and inquiry is all that the petition asks.

I beg leave to add one word more, that may indicate the spirit in which the petition is offered. It is my personal conviction that the inquiry proposed would result in amendments of the Sunday laws in the direction of a larger liberty; that in some details these laws are not conformed to the state of public opinion, nor to the exigencies of modern society, especially in large towns; further, that there are traceable in them some remaining vestiges of an ascetic spirit, and of a disposition to enforce religious duties by law. I should hope to see all such faults radically removed, as the result of the measure sought for in the petition.

I have the honor to be, gentlemen,
With great respect,
Your fellow-citizen,
LEONARD WOOLSEY BACON.

NORWICH, Feb. 28, 1881.

ENFORCEMENT OF SUNDAY LAWS.

SPEECH TO THE CITIZENS OF NORWICH, MONDAY EVENING, AUGUST 11, 1879, JUST AFTER THE PUBLIC DEFIANCE OF THE LAW OF CONNECTICUT SECURING A WEEKLY DAY OF REST.

FELLOW CITIZENS,— Within a few months past, the cities of New London and Norwich have begun to grow accustomed to sights and sounds with which formerly they have been unfamiliar. It has once been a matter of thankfulness to God, of worthy pride in view of the condition of other peoples,— a matter of admiration to thoughtful travellers from foreign lands, that here the first day of the week was a day of rest and quietness. On that day the peace of God settled down over all the land. The din of labor ceased, and the din of strife and of merry-making; and a few quiet hours were given in which the poorest home might be made happy by the gathering of the family, and the most engrossed and toil-burdened soul might at least have its opportunity, if it would, to worship God undisturbed by calls to labor or solicitations to public revelry. This was the glory and beauty of the American, — the New England Sabbath. None felt it so profoundly as those who had grown up in lands where it was unknown. Among those who have come hither from distant parts of the world to study the causes that have given to America her pre-eminence among the nations, and to New England her pre-eminence among the American States, there are few who have not been able to recognize that the American superiority, not merely in moral and social order and in general intelligence, but even in the mere matter of productive industry, was largely due to the institution of the Sabbath calm and rest, as inherited from our fathers, and guarded by law from interruption and abuse. We loved and gloried in our quiet Sunday, and thought of the goodly heritage that should be the birthright of our children.

This glory is departed. I do not say it is endangered. It is *gone*. The New England Sabbath in New London and Norwich within these few months has ceased to be. And whether it has ceased forever is for the citizens of these two towns to say. If they say nothing, and do nothing, within a few weeks more it has ceased forever. Individuals and families and congregations will continue, doubtless, without molestation, or without *much* molestation, to follow their several convictions of duty concerning the day, as Christian families and churches do in heathen countries. But the New England Sabbath as a public institution, guarded by public law from invasion and abuse, is — dead. This revolution, the most momentous, the most disastrous, in our history, will shortly have been accomplished by your acquiescence. And you will be able, by and by, to say to your children, "It was in my day, during my active citizenship, during my pastorship, during my term of public office, and by my dereliction of personal and official duty, that Norwich lost her immemorial glory and privilege of a restful and peaceful Sunday, — that the law on which it depended was suffered to lapse without one effort to assert its dignity and validity, and all for lack of one resolute citizen, and one unflinching official in the right place: it lapsed, not by negligence or evasion or furtive violation, unnoticed, winked at or disregarded, — the law might endure all these and still be law, — it lapsed through the impudent defiance of the law by a petty steamboat corporation, before whose open challenge, 'We intend to violate this statute, and what are you going to do about it?' the citizens held their peace, and the authorities were dumb. Then it was that the law of the quiet Sabbath died; for the law that could be insolently defied by this corporation was incapable of being enforced thereafter against anybody. And when this law was thus insulted, overridden, trampled down, all law suffered with it, and government itself suffered a lasting dishonor. And, to this irreparable damage to our homes and native land, we, by our acquiescence, were parties and accomplices." Go, say this over to yourself as it will sound twenty years hence! Go, take it to your children and grandchildren as a part of the record of your life! Go, rehearse it to yourself as you will give it in at the judgment-seat of God, when you give account of your duty as a citizen! For this is what is meant when, fortnight by fortnight, in open, confessed defiance of the law of the State, the excursion steamer, with public announcement, with its instruments of music, with its private stores of whiskey, and with its complement of prostitutes, waits on Sunday morning at the dock to solicit the company of your children and your brothers and your husbands, and when on Sunday night she vomits out upon the dock again her passengers debauched and drunk;[1] and

[1] "The excursion of the Ella last Sunday was extensively patronized; and many of the participants, before the boat reached her wharf at night, became very boisterous, not to say drunk, thus tending to destroy the quiet enjoyment and rest supposed to be the leading features of a Sunday trip. A perfectly honorable and unprejudiced gentleman of this city, accompanied by his wife, was on board the boat, supposing that the excursionists would at least pay some respect to the day, or, in any event, that the officers of the boat would see that law and order prevailed. He says, that, long before the steamer reached her wharf in this city, he was heartily ashamed of the company in which he found himself, and on no account would he again patronize the craft with her present management on a Sunday excursion. Drunkenness and disorder were quickly visible on board, in the old men as well as the young; and a general hilarity seemed to be diffused among the party. No liquor was sold on the boat, but the thirsty passengers were frequently seen cooling their tongues with hearty draughts from capacious pocket flasks. A company of women from a house near the Norwich and Worcester Depot (of which some

you, meanwhile, sit quietly in your churches and prayer-meetings, and dream of serving God, when, by all the duties he has laid upon you as a citizen, God is calling you to serve him elsewhere and otherwise.

I beg you to remark, that in all that I have said thus far concerning the Sabbath rest, and in all I have yet to say, I have said and shall say no word of it as an institution of God, or

of the 'fathers' have testified that it is a 'quiet and orderly place') were along, and during the day became so exhilarated that one of them had to be led off the boat on her return to this city. The bathing scenes and conduct of this party while at the Hill are also said to have been scandalous. When a party of young gentlemen — so called — induce a comrade who has but recently entered the walks of married life to leave the side of his newly-made bride, despite her expostulations, and, after plying him with liquor, send him back to her drunken and brawling, and then laugh at her tears, it is certainly a question whether or not Sunday excursions are of benefit, especially those of this sort." — *Norwich correspondence of the New Haven Register, Aug. 3, 1879.*

The character of these excursions, infamous as it has been, makes no essential part of my argument. It is quite indifferent to me whether the steamboat company claim that these orgies were an affair of their own, and not to be imputed as an unavoidable incident to a Sunday excursion; or that the company are not to blame because on Sunday excursions such things cannot be helped. This is an affair between the company and its customers, with which the public has little concern. Both parties are "in the same boat."

the subject of a divine command. For I am speaking to you as citizens with reference to your duties to society. The command of God, applying to the individual conscience, has reasons and arguments and sanctions of its own. And, if I could but get the serious attention of that multitude of merry-makers, I would gladly speak to them of God's word and will in this thing, how reasonable and benevolent they are, and, in their true meaning, how far from the austerity that has sometimes been imputed to them or superinduced upon them. But I am not speaking to them about their private duty to God, but to you about your civil duty to the community. And it is not your duty as a citizen to enforce God's law upon your neighbors, but to sustain human law, which God requires men to obey, and citizens to sustain, and magistrates to execute. As a Christian, as a man, you have to do with the Sabbath as a religious institution. As a citizen, you have only to do with it as a civil institution. As a citizen, you are not charged with enforcing the Decalogue, only with sustaining the statute. This is not a religious matter at all, except as it is your religious duty to be faithful to your secular responsibility as a citizen.

You thought, perhaps, that the laws concerning Sunday were laws prescribing a precept of the Christian religion, concerning the obligation of which some consciences might be in doubt. Not at all. What word is there in the statutes that would need to be changed if this country were Buddhist or Confucian or Atheist instead of Christian? What word is there about worship, in the statute, except to provide that it shall not be molested? The law makes no attempt to enforce *religion* upon Sunday. It simply institutes a weekly civil holiday, and surrounds it with safeguards such as the interests of society require. It makes no preamble; it sets up no pretension to divine right in this law, beside the divine right that belongs to every righteous enactment of constituted authority. Nobody denies the competency of the State to establish this weekly holiday; nobody asks to have it abrogated. There are not men enough to call themselves a party, who do not want Sunday maintained by law as a day of rest. Only one business corporation says,

"If only we can do business while all the rest are restrained from it, we shall make a lot of money. We don't want the law repealed. We want it enforced against all other business establishments. We want the shops and factories shut up by law, and the employees compelled to rest. We want other companies to show a decent regard for right and duty. And then what we want for ourselves is to *break* the law. We can influence votes. We can have a mob to clamor for us. We can get demagogues very cheap to howl for the dear people and the poor workingman. We *will* break the law; and touch us if you dare!" And I don't suppose you *do* dare, do you? You would not really have the courage, would you, citizens, magistrates, of Norwich, to oppose a *steamboat company*, when it expected to make a great deal of money by breaking the law? Frankly, I do not believe you would. I have no strong expectation of it on your part.

Allow me to say just here in passing, by way of personal explanation, that I think my position and purpose in this matter have been very much mistaken by the public generally. I don't care for the mistake on my own account, but it seems desirable for the sake of the public that they should understand the matter correctly. It seems to be conceived that I have undertaken to dictate to the people of Norwich how they shall spend their Sundays; and, in particular, that I have started with the resolution and expectation of breaking up the Sunday pleasure excursions of the steamer "Ella," in which some persons wish me success, and the large majority (I judge) prophesy that I shall meet with defeat and disappointment. Now, this is a misconception. I have, in the exercise of my unquestionable rights as a citizen, taken certain steps which may, or may not, result in the stopping of these excursions by the due course of law. If these steps do so result, it will be no affair of mine, and no triumph of mine. If they fail of this result, I shall be neither defeated nor disappointed, nor even surprised. For I have been distinctly warned, from the beginning, that I was entering on a fruitless experiment; that the authorities would not sustain me; that the newspaper would not sustain me; that public opinion would not sustain me; that the law, to which I had referred the matter, could not be enforced. I have gone forward with this distinct understanding. And, if any of you would like to know why I have gone forward, I would like to have you know; and I will tell you, as briefly as possible.

It is almost exactly twelve months ago that a gratifying invitation was pressed upon me to come to Norwich and settle permanently as a minister of the gospel. As I was considering the question, it was represented to me more than once, from various quarters, that Norwich was a place of bad character for crime and lawlessness. (This, of course, was no reason for not coming hither to preach the gospel; although it might be a reason for not bringing one's children with him to be educated here.) From that day to this, I have heard these accusations against the character of the town repeated, publicly and privately, often abroad, sometimes by citizens of high standing at home. I must say that some things have come to my knowledge since my coming here that tend to confirm these reproaches. "Do I mean the Cobb trial?" No, I don't mean the Cobb trial. That is an honor to the character of the town, — not a disgrace. It is not the cases that you try and punish that debase the character of the town and smirch its good name; but the cases that you don't punish, that you don't try, that you don't allow to be tried, that (so the criminal's defenders impudently boast) you don't *dare* to allow to be tried. I have the astounding document in my possession which shows how, in a crime of the blackest turpitude, a blood-guilty felony, in which the criminal was held for trial, the evidence was ready, the prosecuting officers were ready and confident of conviction, the courts were ready, and the law was clear, twoscore of the very best citizens of this town interposed to arrest the course of law, to throw the protection of their personal influence over the criminal, and to condone the crime. Such things as these on the one hand. On the other hand, I need not recount what beautiful and honorable evidences one meets with here, of public spirit and virtue, and of love of law and order. You will not wonder that I was perplexed by the two contrary testimonies, and felt that I would like to know — and I am sure you will not consider it an idle curiosity — I would like to know just what sort of place Norwich was, on this question of law and order. And right here, at hand, is the very opportunity of finding out. I have been hearing, almost ever since I came to the town, the protests of good citizens about the unlawful Sunday excursions that had been lately instituted. People were indignant about them, it was said. Persons high in office characterized them as a nuisance and a shame. A memorial against them, I am told, was signed last year by several hundreds of respectable names. Here, then, was just the case that would show what Norwich was, — whether it was the lawless, crime-breeding place that some alleged, or whether it is a place where good citizens, demanding the enforcement of the laws, can secure it. Now, you will understand what my position is in this matter. I have not undertaken to enforce the Sunday laws. This is not my business. I have not resolved to put a stop to the Sunday excursions. Persons of experience and responsibility tell me it cannot be done, — and perhaps they know. What I have undertaken, in the discharge of my duty as a citizen, — less my duty than that of many others, but mine when all the rest have failed, — is to put this matter in a shape to be tried, and so to find out what sort of a place Norwich is, — what sort of citizens it has, what sort of government it has. And I hope to know in about three weeks.

It is not, then, with any sanguine expectations of a visible, practical result that I press upon you this

(I.) First point, that the fact to which I call your attention is a bold, insolent, defiant violation of the law. We do not raise the question, — we cannot raise the question, — we cannot entertain the question just at this moment, — whether it is a good law, in its particulars, or a bad law. Farther on, I shall have something to say on this point; and by and by, when in a loyal way, as good citizens, they may choose to raise the question of repeal or amendment in due course of legislation, we shall be ready, I am sure, to go into this question thoroughly, and in no unfriendly or illiberal spirit. But, so long as the situation is one of open defiance of the authority of law, we have nothing to do but to try conclusions between law and lawlessness, and find out which is the stronger: and, if we are beaten (as very probably we shall be), amendment or repeal of the law is of the very slightest consequence; for law is dead. The steamboat company is King; the howling demagogue is its prime minister; the mob is its standing army; and we, who never were in bondage to any man, are its subjects. If this be so, we want to know it; and we therefore make our contention on this single point. This is the law. We claim, we demand, — no, I will not presume too far, for I do not know where you stand in this matter, — *I* claim and *I* demand the enforcement of it as my right as a citizen. And I expect to be refused if law-abiding and law-sustaining citizens are only timid enough, and the government is inactive and unfaithful enough, and the steamboat corporation is bold enough and disloyal enough, and the baser sort are clamorous enough, and ignorant enough of their own interests.

And now, having defined our one main issue, we are in a position to add,

(II.) In the second place, that it is an aggravation of the offence of these open and defiant law-breakers, that they are attacking a *good* and *salutary* law. I speak, not from the religious point of view, but from the point of view of any good citizen, when I say that the particular laws now defied are, in general, good and salutary laws, — laws of inexpressible value to every interest of society and every class of society. *In general*, I say; for it is obvious that these ancient statutes do require amendment in detail to fit them to circumstances and conditions that did not exist when they were made, to the requirements of large towns and modern society. And, whenever it is decided that law can be enforced, I, for one, shall gladly join in seeking the amendment of them. If it is decided, on the other hand, that the law can be successfully defied, it is merely frivolous to talk of amending or repealing or enacting at all. The Legislature, on this subject, may be interesting to the public as a debating-society; but the public has no other interest in its proceedings.

What, then, is the inexpressible value to the public of these laws which are now defied? This: that they guarantee to the whole community that which could not exist without them,—a public day of rest. If this should be lost, the community in all its classes, but most of all in its poorer classes, will lament it with long, perhaps with unavailing, regret. But if these laws are successfully defied, and so broken down, your day of rest *is* lost; for it is only by virtue of these laws that the day of general public rest subsists. A weekly day of rest is the universal desire. Every man, woman, and child wants it, and would feel personally aggrieved and injured if it should be taken away. And the way in which this universal desire is secured to all, is by means of a law on the statute-book, which (however it may be neglected or evaded in some cases) stands on the statute-book in full vigor, and is ready to be enforced when the case requires, and is actually enforced whenever a single citizen, however humble and however solitary, demands the enforcement of it as his right, and insists upon his demand, as I do insist to-night.

But I am ready to meet the objection which some of you have it at your tongue's end to put: "What is the need of a law to secure what everybody wants? If everybody wants it, will it not come of itself? Will not the unanimous desire of the people, that one day of the week be kept free from the encroachments of business, be a sufficient security for this without the aid of law?"

I answer, Yes; just so much as the unanimous desire of the property owners on Main Street would, without law, preserve the line of the street from encroachments,—just so much, and no more. It is the general interest of the whole property, and every part of it, on both sides of the way, that the width of that street should not be reduced. You could get a remonstrance, signed by every person in the city that could hold a pen, against permitting owners of frontage on that street to build out on it a single foot; and all the owners themselves would join in the remonstrance. What is the need of any law, then, to protect the line of that street? If everybody wants it, it will take care of itself, won't it? And yet there is not a man of you that knows how to pretend to be so dull as not to see that it is only by the force of law that the object of the unanimous desire can be secured, — a law ready to be enforced, actually enforced on demand, and that cannot be defied. There may be furtive and casual violations of the law: these may be overlooked and neglected, and the law will not lose its force thereby, nor the rights of the public be impaired. But let there be one man or one corporation sufficiently strong, rich, influential of votes, and sufficiently insolent and unscrupulous to say, and say successfully, "I am going to build out three feet in my front, and what are you going to do about it?" — let but one humble citizen make his complaint to authorities and courts in vain, and the line of your street is gone. Encroachment will follow encroachment, the encroachment of one excusing and necessitating the encroachment of his neighbor, until the thoroughfare is choked, and the interest of all has been defeated by the selfishness of one. And allow me to add here (for it meets an objection that may impose on some minds), that it makes no difference at all whether the citizen complaining, and complaining in vain, of the infraction of the public right, is personally injured, or whether anybody is actually injured, by this particular encroachment, or whether the complaint is made out of solicitude for the future welfare of the town. Suppose, even, that the encroachment pretends to be for the public convenience, — that the benevolent citizen proposes to build a drinking fountain in front of his shop, for instance; so long as the encroachment is made without law, against law, and in successful defiance of the law, invoked for its removal, it is all the same. The law is down, and the street-line is broken for everybody.

The analogy is strong, and holds at all points. The great common rest, opened by a beneficent statute in the midst of the toil of the week, is like the village green reserved for public refreshment and delight amid the bustling streets of a New England village, sacred from the invasion of business, where the children of the rich and poor may play alike, where the sacred graves of other generations wake tender thoughts and holy memories, and amongst them the church of Christ invites to prayer and praise, —

"And points with taper spire to heaven."

The whole people want it: everybody is willing to respect it, on condition that everybody else shall be required to respect it too. Only, if there is to be no law about it, and these immemorial rights of the public are to be left open to a general scramble, in which the earliest squatter on the public privilege will get the best advantage and the biggest share, then it is too much to hope from human nature that the scramble will not begin.

Fellow-citizens, the scramble has begun. An insolent corporation has squatted on your old graveyard, and is digging the foundation for his money-making shop among the bones of your fathers. It may be difficult for you to deal with him; but, if you give it up, it will be impossible for you ever to deal with any other. We propose — *I* propose — to try the strength of the public law against this intruder on our common rest. If we fail, as it seems to me somewhat likely that we shall, in a year or two we shall have competing lines of excursion steamers, advertising their rival attractions in "The Bulletin" (with an encouraging notice from the editor, of course); and you will wish you could stop it, but you can't. By and by the railroad companies will enter into the business, with new attractions on the bill; and you will wish you could stop them, but you can't. Not very long hence, the same argument, the necessity of recreation for the poor workingman, which requires a Sunday excursion in summer, will be found to require a Sunday afternoon and evening variety theatre — a quiet and well-conducted variety theatre — in the winter. And you will ache under the infliction, and wish you could abolish it; but you can't. Your law is dead; and you, perhaps, have helped to murder it.

This is not all. The man who finds now that he can make money on Sunday with his steamboat, will find before long, if times improve and orders crowd him, that he can make money on Sunday by running his factory. And he will do it, — quietly, of course, but he'll do it. And why shouldn't he? You cannot stop him then. Now you can, by law. But he is to defy and break down the law that holds him back. Society will lament in all its ranks, and most of all in its ranks of honest workingmen, that the blessed common rest is gone, — stolen, — no, there is no stealth about it, — openly robbed away, before the face of the citizen and the law, and that now there may be seven working-days in the week at the discretion of the corporation or contractor; and you will mourn the day when you were tickled by the offer of a cheap excursion, or bullied by the insolence of a steamboat corporation, into giving up this priceless heritage of the American workingman; and you will long and long that you could get back your one day of rest in seven. But you can't.

This is not all. Let it go abroad in all the papers that the Sunday law in all these towns has been successfully defied, and about how many weeks do you think it will be before some gentleman from New York, with a foreign accent, and a small stock of fancy goods, will open a little store on Main Street, for a few weeks only, and will let it be understood that it will be open, with half a shutter down, on Sunday afternoons, after the hours of service, for the benefit of the poor workingmen and working-women who really haven't any day but Sunday for quiet shopping. You won't like this, you storekeepers on the same street; but you cannot stop it. And, what is more, you will have to fall in with it sooner or later, or retire from business. You will try to make a combination against it at first; but one after another will begin to break ranks, and send just one clerk for the Sunday business. By and by the understanding will be that each clerk may be at liberty every second Sunday, or at least one Sunday in every month. The strong and respectable firms will hold out a long time against the new way. They will come into it, slowly, reluctantly; but they will come into it. They will have to, or sell out.

All this is not coming at once. The force of religious principle and the force of habit will retard it. And this is the very fact over which these law-breakers are inwardly chuckling as they count their fortnightly gains. They don't want it to come all at once. The longer the better. What they want is, that everybody else should be forced to suspend his business, so as to make customers for theirs. Work presses you hard in your shop or store, and there are not days enough in the week for what you can profitably do. But Saturday night shuts down; and the law says to you and to your neighbor, and to all your competitors in business, Rest there. And all the wheels of society and commerce are still, and the blessed truce of God comes down like a benediction, and the world is at peace. And now into the midst of this serene and beautiful calm comes snarling in the insolent whistle of the steamboat company, saying, "I'll break all this. The law shall bind you, but it shan't bind me. My disloyalty shall grow rich and fat on your obedience to law. What do I care for you, or your antiquated laws? What do I care what the effect is going to be on Norwich five years hence, or one year hence. I make my money now. I am going to do as I please about it; and touch me, if you dare!" And, so far as I am able to judge at present, you don't dare.

There ought to be authority — there *is* authority, there ought to be power, will, and courage, *with* authority — to take this public robber of the public privileges by the throat, and shake him in the grip of the law until he shall let go his felon's hold upon your rights and mine. I am not blaming or accusing the government and officers of this city for their action or non-action in the matter. They understand the ground, and I don't. They know how strong the steamboat company is, and whether it is stronger against the law than they are with the law. No man, no officers, ought to be blamed for not doing that which is simply an impossibility. Perhaps it is true that government is not strong enough in Norwich, that there is not enough of public virtue in the citizens behind it, that there is too formidable a force of lawlessness in front of it, for it to be possible to execute the law against the law-breaker. Perhaps this is true. This is what people say about you; and this is the ground that seems to be taken by leading citizens, official and unofficial, with whom I have conversed. Perhaps it is true. One thing I happen to know, however, remotely bearing on the subject, which I merely mention as a matter of incidental interest. *This isn't so at New London.* I happen to know, on entirely satisfactory evidence, that in that city they have a public sentiment high enough, and a government strong enough, and a mayor, — his name is Thomas Waller, of the Democratic party; and I wish he would move to Norwich, so that I might have the opportunity of voting for him for something, — a mayor who is brave and resolute and wilful enough to meet and handle any law-breaker, even a steamboat company. I am not blaming you here. I am not casting censure on the officials of the city. Perhaps the case is different in Norwich, and this cannot be done here. That is the thing that people say about you, and that is the thing that I am intending to find out.

These laws for the protection of Sunday, — Blue Laws, as they are called by those who take pleasure in insulting the memory of their own fathers, and the character of their native State, by repeating the hundred-times-exploded calumnies of an old and malignant libel, — these ancient statutes, antiquated in phraseology and details, and plainly requiring amendment to suit them to conditions of society unknown at the time of their enactment, are yet, as I have said, of priceless value as securing to every man, what he could not have without them, his weekly day of rest. They are of like value for another reason, which I can hardly do more than mention, though it is not of less importance than the first.

These laws create a universal public holiday; and a public holiday is a public peril. A necessity it may be, — it is; but the history of all nations shows it to be a dangerous necessity. The State which by positive enactment institutes this dangerous blessing, striking off all the common restraints of regular industry, is bound to guard it to the utmost from abuse. The State has a perfect right to make a holiday; but it has no right to make a holiday, and take no precautions against the mischiefs that tend to result from it. It has no right with one hand to lock the doors of the factory, the shop, the school, against honest industry and useful pursuits, and turn the business population into the street, and then with the other hand fling wide the enticing portals of temptation. The authority that has the right to say to the capitalist, or the corporation, or the contractor, you shall not exact labor on that day, has a right to say, and is bound to say, to the speculator in amusements, you shall not start a carousal or a show or an excursion on that day. Wives and mothers have a right to demand that the beneficent law which makes it possible for Sunday to be a day of blessed domestic happiness, shall be attended by provisions that shall guard it from becoming a terror and a curse, — a day when they shall sit the long hours through in trembling, lest at night those whom they love shall be tumbled in upon them through the street-door, drunk, — that the state shall not loose the iron band of industry without at the same time tightening the rein of salutary law. Our great productive and commercial industries have rights in the matter. They know the financial loss there is in a disordered Sabbath; and, if they are wise, they will take their stand at the door of the City Hall, alongside of the workmen whose liberty of weekly rest is menaced by the insolence of a law-defying corporation, and demand, in a voice not to be disregarded, that the State, which interferes to take their employees out of business on Saturday night, shall also interfere to save them from being returned to business on Monday morning exhausted, demoralized, debauched.

Observe, now, the two points which we have reached. We have placed our main contention on this simple point, that the act in question is a defiant and insolent violation of law.

Then, secondly, we have noted it as an aggravation of the offence, that the law which it violates and openly threatens to nullify and destroy is a good and salutary law, of priceless value to society, to every interest of society, to every member of society, rich or poor, high or low.

I beg you now,

(III.) To note, as a further aggravation of the

offence, the vile dishonesty, hypocrisy, and cant with which it is endeavored to apologize for the offence. This unlawful speculation of a greedy steamboat company is, forsooth, a *philanthropic* undertaking. It is devised by the friends of the workingman — the poor workingman — the dear workingman. The poor, dear workingman is persecuted by a lot of straight-laced Puritans, of stern, hard, cold-hearted religionists, of overbearing, domineering parsons and deacons, who are resolved that the poor, dear workingman shall have no chance to enjoy himself on his one only holiday. But poor workingmen, dear workingmen, don't you be afraid. The steamboat company will stand by you. The steamboat company is the poor man's friend. We will protect you in your right to your holiday, — your only holiday. Come right aboard, and don't be afraid. And mind you have your — a — your — well, so to speak, your *change* ready at the captain's office. The fare is extremely cheap, for it is quite a philanthropic enterprise.

Shame on this pack of snivelling lies! How came the American workingman to *have* this one holiday in every week? Answer me that! Who gave to the American, the Connecticut workingman, this peculiar privilege, this royal inheritance, and guaranteed it by all the authority of the commonwealth,—the priceless possession of an inviolable Sabbath rest, his own, his glory, that sets him without a peer among the workingmen of almost all the world beside, and makes him at once their admiration and their envy? How did he come by it? To whom does he owe it? Well, strangely enough, it appears on inquiry that he owes it to that implacable enemy, the straight-laced Puritan! And what is his sole defence and guaranty of the inviolability of this sacred right against the irrestrainable rapacity of competing business interests? Nothing in the world but these despised, antiquated, derided, and scoffed-at statutes,—these "blue laws," which you talk so merrily of throwing overboard as obsolete and preposterous, and incapable of being enforced. And who is it that is threatening to break down the safeguards of the one secure and quiet refuge for exhausted toil, to tear away the walls of legal enactment that guard the Sabbath rest? Oh, this is the strangest thing of all! for, come to look him in the face, he turns out to be none other than the poor workingman's, the dear workingman's, the poor, dear workingman's, affectionate friend, — the liberal and philanthropic steamboat company.

Workingmen of Norwich, don't be fooled! Think twice over it, and look at the bargain on both sides, before you make up your minds to trade off your birthright for this miserable mess of pottage that the benevolent steamboat company are stirring up for you. But if you find these corporation blandishments too alluring, and the savor of their somewhat strong-scented excursions too charming to be resisted, then remember, by and by, the warning I give you beforehand, that the time is not far off when you will find the little finger of an unrestricted corporation to be heavier than the loins of a Puritan statute. It seems to you very fine when Mr. Paul Greene snaps his fingers in the face of the prosecuting officer, and steams down the river, blowing his impudent steamboat whistle in the ears of Christian congregations assembled for the worship of Almighty

God, and asks derisively the famous question of that other poor man's friend, Mr. William Tweed, "What are you going to do about it?" This is very fine indeed, and shows a noble independence of the laws of the State. But I would just advise you to think ahead a little, and fancy how it is going to sound to you, three or four years hence, when the benevolent Mr. Paul Greene's *factory whistle* (if he has one) wakes you up before daylight on a Sunday morning, with a hint that you are wanted in the mill, and that, if you have any objections or scruples about working on Sunday, he can find somebody else in your place; and "what are you going to do about it?" And hadn't you better be getting your answer ready in advance? What *are* you going to do about it? You will begin to talk about the law and your rights. And the workingman's friend will tell you, "The law! that ridiculous old blue law is played out long ago. Don't you remember the jolly Sunday excursions we used to have on 'The Ella,' all for the benefit of the poor workingman?" And what will you say then? You will not *say* much, I suspect; but you will begin to wish in your heart that when Mr. Paul Greene invited you to join him in breaking down the old Sunday law, you had taken the precaution to ask him what sort of Sunday law he was going to give you in the place of it.

I have detained this vast throng of people a long time already, but it is absolutely necessary that I should say a few words in answer to the one solitary objection of the slightest weight that I have heard alleged against the enforcement of this law against the Sunday pleasure-excursions of the steamer "Ella." The objection is this: that the law is so worded as to be capable of vexatious, annoying, malicious applications; to which it is sometimes added by those who think they know, that these annoying and malicious applications will certainly be made, vindictively, on the part of the steamboat company in case it is interfered with.

Undoubtedly the objection is not without ground. Our statutes date from a period before the existence among us of large towns with their peculiar requirements, and of modern conveniences of transportation, that have grown almost or quite into necessities. The law, if rigorously enforced, might require some transportation companies to revise their time-tables (which does not strike me as an evil), and might perhaps (though this is doubtful) interfere to an injurious extent with the street-car and omnibus service. Some such inconveniences as this would have to be endured until the law should be amended. I have no doubt that society would be able to bear up under the burden for a few months.

The answer to this objection is already given, and it is an overwhelming one. Over against the petty inconveniences that *may* result from enforcing the law, I set the enormous, the almost infinite loss that inevitably *will* result to society if the law is successfully defied; and there I leave that matter.

It is the remark of no religious zealot, but of one of the coolest and shrewdest students of practical politics, the late Horace Greeley, in one of his letters from Europe, that we in America are shut up to the choice between the Puritan Sabbath and the Parisian Sabbath. This issue is now before you, citizens; and in a few more weeks, whatever you may do or not do, the decision will have been made.

Before the matter is irrevocably settled by your action or your inaction, I could wish you might stand with me an hour on Sunday morning in the "labor-market" at Geneva, and see the troops of dull, tired, sodden-looking laborers, in their ragged blouses, unwashed from the grime and sweat of one week's work, trudging off sluggishly and wearily, "like dumb, driven cattle," to the work of the next week. Are these slaves? you ask. Slaves! Bless you, no, my dear man! These are freemen. These are voters and citizens in a land of universal suffrage, under the freest government on earth, with an advanced and liberal constitution of the latest French invention and with all the modern improvements. No "blue laws" here: they had blue laws once in Geneva (though they never did in Connecticut), but they have laughed them down long ago. This, which you see, is liberty,—complete, untrammelled liberty. Every one of these free citizens has a right—a proud, inviolable right—to work on Sunday if he chooses. And this is what it ends in for him;

and this is where it will end for you, if you choose to make the costly experiment. The workingman who MAY work on Sunday, when work is wanted has GOT to work on Sunday. FOR THE LIBERTY OF REST FOR EACH ONE DEPENDS ON A LAW OF REST FOR ALL.

Think of it! Think of it twice! Think of it again! and then say whether you will barter away your birthright, the American Sunday, the universal privilege of rich and poor, for this miserable French delusion, a Parisian holiday, through which one half the people are condemned to toil, that the other half may frolic.

I have done. I stand before you here a solitary citizen, with not one influential friend at my back, to state this case to you, as I have already stated it to the prosecuting officer and to the executive officers of the city. The prosecuting officer will do his duty: he has no option in the case.[1] The mayor will do his duty, I have not the slightest doubt, according to his conscientious understanding of it.

[1] This turned out to be a mistake. When it came to the scratch, the attorney flinched.

Whether you will do your duty or not I do not know. I have delivered my soul. On every hand, as I walk the streets, I hear nothing but presages of defeat, with expressions sometimes of exultation, sometimes of sympathy. Exult, I beg you, to your hearts' content, but save your sympathies till they are wanted. I cannot be defeated. You may be defeated. But I defy the world and the Devil to defeat me, for my work is done. I have dragged these two most reluctant parties together, — the Law and the Law-breakers, — and compelled them to stand face to face in the civil forum and in the forum of the public. Henceforth, it is no fight of mine, although my rights and liberties as well as yours are at stake in it. But I shall stand by and watch the progress of it; and shortly I shall know, and the State shall know, and the land shall know, what is the character of Norwich as a law-abiding, law-sustaining, law-enforcing city.

II.

SIX SERMONS ON THE SABBATH QUESTION.

By GEORGE BLAGDEN BACON.

PREFACE.

THIS book is simply what it pretends to be, a series of sermons preached to the author's own congregation. He has preferred to print them unaltered; adding, however, occasional references in the form of foot-notes. And, if the book shall seem to be needlessly diffuse or unduly rhetorical in its style, it is only just to remember that it was designed to be spoken, not to be read.

It is not probable that there is any thing new in the argument herein presented. Indeed, it is scarcely possible to say any thing new on a subject which has been so long and so thoroughly discussed. But the argument for the observance of the Lord's Day, as these sermons present it, is not the one to which the American churches are in the habit of listening; and it therefore had the merit of freshness to most of those who heard it. Moreover, the discussion seemed to be timely, in view of recent agitations of "the Sunday question" in New York and New Jersey; and some persons found it useful in the relief of perplexities by which their minds had been troubled. Others, hesitating fully to accept the argument, desired the opportunity to examine it more carefully. The volume is, therefore, printed especially for the use of those to whom the sermons were first preached.

But it is believed that the wider publication of it may be useful. For there are many Christian people, who, while greatly approving and even adopting what has been called the "Anglo-American" practice with regard to the Lord's Day, have never been satisfied with the theory which influential writers in England and America have supposed to be essential to that practice. And it is not pleasant for those who are thus honestly obliged to differ from their brethren, to find themselves put, even by implication, outside of the number of "evangelical Christians," and to be told that the opinions which they hold are "defective, erroneous, and worthless," or "productive of extreme mischief," [1] or the like. Against such "judgment of the brethren," to which there seems to be a constant tendency, not only on the part of individuals, but even on the part of corporations, this volume may serve as a timely protest.

[1] See Gilfillan's The Sabbath. American Tract Society's edition, pp. 576, 577.

For though that protest has been often made, and with the sanction of most venerable and authoritative names, it needs to be repeated constantly. And just now it will be a useful encouragement to some perplexed consciences to be reminded, that, if they must hold such views as those herein set forth, they can hold them without sin.

For this reason, among others, and because it is believed that these views are really, as they were honestly designed to be, in the interest of the better observance of the Lord's Day, they receive a publication which was not at first intended for them.

THE SABBATH QUESTION.

I.

THE SABBATH OF GOD.

"Thus the heavens and the earth were finished, and all the host of them. And on the seventh day God ended his work which he had made; and he rested on the seventh day from all his work which he had made. And God blessed the seventh day, and sanctified it: because that in it he had rested from all his work which God created and made." — GEN. ii. 1-3.

IT is impossible to turn these earliest pages of the Hebrew Scriptures without peculiar interest, in which there is mingled something of irrepressible reverence. If for no other reason than their extreme antiquity, then for that, they are sufficiently venerable. But they challenge our reverence not for that only; the themes with which they are occupied are of such sublime importance, and the statements which they make are uttered with such simplicity, such dignity, such poetic beauty, such philosophic wisdom, that we cannot read them without increasing wonder and deepening veneration. Puzzled we may often be, in our endeavors to interpret them; perplexed by the apparent contradictions which we find in them, when we compare them with the records discovered by the researches of science; forced to reject old explanations, and to take up with new hypotheses concerning them; but we cannot treat them with contempt or with indifference. We may discover that they are not what we at first thought they were, — that they are not, in all cases, to be taken literally, — that in matters strictly scientific they are probably not authoritative; but if we should, therefore, infer that the world has outgrown these first chapters of the Book of Genesis, and can afford to disregard them, we should make a very serious mistake indeed.

For if these pages do not teach us geology, as we used to think they did, they teach us something better and more valuable than geology. If they do not teach us chronology, they teach us truth of more eternal interest than chronology. They assert some things concerning God, and some things concerning man, which it is of the profoundest importance that we should know and ponder, — things which are fundamental to all true religious thought and to all high religious activity. The revelation of a personal God, and of man as made in the image of God, — if these first pages of Genesis declared no other truths than these, still they would be of most incalculable value. One God, from whom are all things; one man, made in the image of God, — these are the two prime facts which lie at the foundation of the world's history. God and man, — these are the two great actors in that history. The relation of God to man, the relation of likeness, — though at an infinite distance, yet real likeness notwithstanding, — this is what makes possible a science of theology. The relation of man to God, a relation which makes possible some reciprocity of affection, this, I might almost say, is the very definition of religion. Such considerations as these will show us why it is that these first pages of the Bible are not to be discarded as if obsolete and worthless.

There seems to be another truth, of profound interest and value, — a truth somehow grounded upon this relation between God and man, — hinted at in the verses which I have chosen for our text. It will not be easy, perhaps, to draw it forth, and state it in such a way as shall convey no false impression. The work of explaining these first chapters of Genesis is not at all easy. We read of God as working six days, to create the heavens and the earth, and resting on the seventh. And we find some parallel drawn between God and man, as working and as resting. And all sorts of questions occur to us, — questions which it is much easier to ask than to answer. What are these six days in which God wrought these works? What is this seventh day in which he rested from them? What is his work? What is his rest? Is he, then, ever tired? Or is he ever idle? And what analogy can there be between such words as "work" and "rest" applied to God, and the same words applied to man?

And yet analogy of some sort seems to be hinted. Here is this mysterious assertion that our human nature is somehow in the image of

God; and here is the observance of rest, on our part, grounded on the fact that God himself rested, and sanctified and blessed the day on which he rested. Surely there is something to be learned concerning our own duty, concerning our own privilege, concerning that "rest" spoken of in the Epistle to the Hebrews[1] (or, as it stands in the original,[2] that "keeping of Sabbath"), which "remaineth for the people of God," if we can learn what God's own Sabbath, of which this text speaks, signified, and wherein it consisted.

Let us rather say "consists" and "signifies," — using the present tense, and not the past. For I believe, and I shall try to show, that God's Sabbath still continues. Need we insist, — nay, even can we suppose, that the seventh day, which God blessed and sanctified, was really a day of twenty-four hours' duration, according to the measure of a man's comprehension? If the six days which preceded it were, as used to be supposed, six literal days of twenty-four hours each, then this also should be such. But if, as science tells us, and as

---

[1] Chaps. ii. and iv.   [2] Chap. iv. 17.

Christian scholars all agree, it was not through six brief days, but through six mighty epochs of innumerable years, that this work of creation was perfected; if, through ages upon ages, and with catastrophe after catastrophe, and by mighty agencies of fire and frost and flood, God wrought the finished order of his perfect universe, until at last it was made ready for the man created in his image, — if this is true, then we should fitly and naturally expect the seventh day to be a long, vast epoch like the others.

Concerning the six ages of creation, there is not any longer room for doubt. There was a time — not so very long ago — when good men imagined, that, unless they contended for the literal exactness of this narrative in Genesis, they were surrendering the very fortress of revealed religion, and undermining the very foundation of the truth. And so they did contend for literal days, and literal mornings and literal evenings to each one, and each one twenty-four literal hours in length, no more, no less; contended vehemently as for essential truth; contended in the face of science; contended in contempt of all the testimony which God had written in the book of nature; contended even in conflict with the coherent story of the Book of Genesis itself. But this is no longer thought necessary; nor is it any longer deemed heresy, if we interpret the scriptural record by the commentary of the records in the rocks. And the result of this interpretation is, that distinct and successive periods in the process of creation, occurring in the general order indicated in scripture, are indeed discovered in geological history; but, instead of being periods of twenty-four hours, they must have been periods of prolonged and almost incalculable duration. Each one was preceded by a night of darkness, convulsion, catastrophe;[1] and, when

---

[1] The most recent statement of scholarly interpretation on this point may be found in Lange's Commentary on Genesis, issued in the American edition since this sermon was preached. It is quoted because it is the most recent, and because it gives with sufficient completeness the theory of the creative "evenings."

"We are not to conceive of the evening and morning of the single creative days as merely symbolic intervals of the day of God. According to the analogy of the first day, the evening is the time of a peculiar chaotic fermentation of things; while the morning is the time of that new, fair, solemn world-building that corresponds to it. With each evening there is also indicated a new birth-travail of things, a

one night ended, a new order of creation was produced, — and then another night of fire or cataclysm came, and then another day; and so on from stage to stage, until at last, into the world which had been fitted up, by these successive acts, for human habitation and discipline, the man, made in the image of God, was introduced. And the evening of convulsion and darkness, and the morning of new creative forms and phases, made up each one of these immense primeval days. Only, whereas of the first and second, and of all the six, there is recorded a beginning and an end, there is no end recorded of the seventh. What if it be not ended yet? What if the Sabbath which began when the creative work was finished, has continued and is still continuing, and shall still continue while the created universe en-

new earth revolution, which elevates the old formation that went before it, — a seeming darkening, a seeming sunset, or going down of the world. . . . With each morning, on the contrary, there is a new, a higher, a fairer, and a richer state of the world. In this way do the evening and morning in the creative periods have the highest significance for an agreement of the sacred geology with the results of the scientific geology." — LANGE, Genesis, American edition, p. 167.

dures! Each one of those creation days was ages long: is the Sabbath day any shorter? Has it ever been broken in upon by any new creative act? Is not this age of human history, of human discipline, of human sanctification, God's Sabbath age? Is it not this which he has blessed and sanctified?

I know that it is not wise nor safe to speculate concerning questions about which we know so little, — but this inquiry is not one of simply speculative interest. There is a parallel drawn in scripture between God's Sabbath and man's Sabbath, between God's rest and man's rest. Indeed, the one is made the ground of the other. And they are the same in kind. Sabbath is rest. When we know wherein the rest of God consists, we may know wherein our rest is to consist. When we discover what God's Sabbath is, we may discover what our own Sabbath is, or what it ought to be. And I insist, therefore, that the study which we are pursuing this morning is not fanciful or unreasonable.

Assuming, then, for the sake of argument, what it is the duty of those who doubt it to disprove, that the seventh day which God has blessed and sanctified is even now continuing, let us reverently ask how he is spending it. I speak as if it were a mere assumption for the sake of argument; although, if so, it is an assumption which the writer of the Epistle to the Hebrews also makes, when he speaks of the rest into which God has entered as if still continuing, and as being the very same into which a promise is left us of entering also. So that the case stands thus: God began to rest; God never has ceased to rest; God even speaks of his own rest as a continuous and permanent state, in which men may share. "My rest; my rest!" The words are solemnly quoted over and over again by the writer of that Epistle, as full of most profound and awful meaning. The rest of God, the Sabbath of God; not many rests, but one rest; not many Sabbaths, but one Sabbath; not a rest which comes and goes, but a rest which remains,—perpetual, eternal, —this is the true Sabbath. It is God's Sabbath, and it is our Sabbath also if we do not refuse it. What is it, then? How does God spend it? Wherein does it consist?

Not, at any rate, in idleness or inactivity.

We have Christ's own word for that. There has been such a conception of God as that, having made the world and started it in motion, he lets it spin forever, unheeded and unsustained except by some inherent energy of its own; but this is not the Christian conception of God. To loll upon Olympus, to look down in idle unconcern upon the changing scenes of earth, to exist in selfish sloth from age to age, — this was a heathen view of God, and a most gross and false conception of divine blessedness. The God and Father of our Lord Jesus Christ, the one God, the true God, the living God, is no such being as that. "My Father worketh hitherto, and I work," said our Lord in that sublime discourse of his concerning the Sabbath.[1] "You accuse me," says he to the Jews, "you accuse me of working on the Sabbath day; so I do; so does my Father: work is not a violation of the Sabbath; idleness is not an observance of it: my Father is at rest, but he is not idle. My Father worketh hitherto, and I work."

These are divine words. They are too won-

[1] John v. 17.

derful for human philosophies; they are high, we could not attain unto them with our unaided imaginations. Perfectly to grasp the paradox of a God forever busy, yet at rest forever, — of a God in infinite repose, and yet in infinite activity, — only he who spake as never man spake was able. And yet the paradox is true: we feel the truth of it, and do homage to it, even if we cannot explain it. For if God were indeed idle (as a German writer has beautifully said), no sun would shine, no flowers would bloom, all creation would languish, all the universe would dissolve. He is at rest, and yet he makes the outgoing of every morning and every evening to rejoice; every singing-bird pipes because he gladdens it; every sparrow flies because he bears it up; every lily grows because he nurtures it; every hair of every humblest head is numbered by his knowledge. He is at rest, and yet the work of his preserving care continues. He creates no longer; but he sustains, preserves, perpetuates his work.

But much more than this. God enters now upon a higher work; not a work of force, but a work of love. He has to save the man whom he has made. He has to save and sanctify him; and through the long ages of his Sabbath he has patiently been working out, and still is patiently working out, the spiritual perfectness of man. Herein, indeed, we find his Sabbath work. In six days he made the heavens and the earth, and all the host of them, and fitted up man's dwelling-place, and put man in it. On the seventh he is making all things over, making all things new. On the sixth day he made man, on the seventh he is making him a new creature; on the sixth day he made man good, on the seventh he is making him holy; on the sixth day that which is natural, on the seventh day that which is spiritual.

And so the rest of God is seen to be the rising from a lower to a higher work, a ceasing from the work of making to the nobler employment of saving, a passing from his miracles of power to his sublimer miracles of grace! God made the seventh day holy,—blessed it and sanctified it. When the scripture says he sanctified it, it does not merely mean that he called it holy, but that he made it holy. Hitherto in God's creation there had been no chance for holiness. Matter cannot be holy: God could see the material world, that it was good; but he could not see that it was holy: there is no moral quality at all in it. He saw the light, that it was good, — but not that it was holy; so the firmament was good, and the earth, and the waters, and the vegetable world, and the changeful orbs of heaven, and the creeping things of water, and flying fowls of air, and mighty beasts of earth, — all these were good; and man himself, as first of all the animal world, as sum and chief of these created things, was good, but even he, as yet, not holy. The innocence in which man was made was a different thing from holiness. Holiness cannot be created. It is not the result of force. It is the work of liberty. Power can create. But only love can sanctify. The earth and the heavens and all the host of them could be spoken into being by the sovereign will of God, and fashioned through the silent ages by his hands. And man, the summit of creation, could be formed, a living soul, with powers like God's own powers, with liberty like God's. But now, if the problem is to make the man employ his liberty for good and not for evil, use his powers for right and not for wrong, if, in a word, the work is to make this free man a holy man, — this is a work, not for creative force, but for renewing love; not for might like that which heaved the heavens above the spacious earth; not for power like that which fixed the bounds of earth and seas, but for the still, strong Spirit of the living, loving God.

Through six mighty ages, then, in slow succession, was creation perfected; and it was very good. At the head of it, made lord over it, with dominion over all the works of the Creator's hands, stood man, formed in God's image, — free with the dangerous liberty to choose right or to choose wrong, — free in the balanced equipoise of his imperial will. What the Creator's hand can do for him is done. He is made free to act, able to act. If he is forced to act either in one way or in the other, compelled to choose either for right or for wrong, his freedom is destroyed, and his holiness is impossible. Holiness upon compulsion is not holiness. Virtue produced by force is not virtue at all. Right action which is the result of power has not the blessedness which God designs for man. There is no longer room for the creative hand upon man. God has made him, but now himself must act. The six days' work in his behalf is finished. The seventh is begun. In the work of creation God has nothing more to do: scripture and science are at one on this point. This seventh age of human history is consecrated to a nobler work: God has blessed it and sanctified it. He has devoted it to making holy the man whom he made free.

This is the way in which God spends his Sabbath. He creates no longer. But he sanctifies and saves. And so it is not a mere fancy if we discover how, as the six days that preceded it began, each one with evening, even with the darkness of convulsion and catastrophe and almost of chaos come again, — so this seventh day began with evening, even with the night of sin. The man made free to act, chose to act wrong. The image of his Maker was defaced and marred. The whole creation shared the shock and damage of that evil choice. Darkness came upon the earth, — the darkness of a dreadful ruin, — and gross darkness on the people, even the moral darkness of a deadly sin. The whole creation groaned and travailed in the pain and bondage which that bad choice wrought. The night of sin began this Sabbath day.

But presently the day-star rose, the day-star from on high that visited us, — the bright and morning star, the Sun of righteousness. The dawn began in Eden with the promise to the man who sinned. It brightened till the Sun arose at Bethlehem. It shineth more and more unto the perfect day. It is the light of the glory of God shining in Jesus Christ, our Lord. The work of this, the last, the Sabbath day, is to bless and make holy what the six days had created. And the evening and the morning are the seventh day.

But no night shall follow this. This sun which has arisen never shall go down. The gates of this eternal Sabbath shall not be shut at all by day, for there shall be no night there. And the rest whereinto God has entered, and whence his influence of love goes forth to sanctify and save the world, — the rest whereinto

Christ has entered, and whence his loving presence issues with perpetual power to comfort and to help, — the rest into which we are entering by his grace and through his Spirit, — this rest remaineth, though the earth and heaven should pass away. This is the Sabbath. And of this all other days are shadowy and imperfect types. They vanish. This endures.

So we find in the Apocalypse the supplement of Genesis. And if any man has ever wondered why no more is said in the scriptures concerning the seventh day, I tell him that the whole Bible is the history of the seventh day. To it the six days were preliminary. Beside the splendor of its saving grace, the skill and power of those creative eras dwindle. When God ceased from forming worlds, and fashioning their myriad inhabitants, it was to sanctify and bless. His highest rest is holiness; and holiness with him is not an idle and inactive being good, but a perpetual and busy and self-sacrificing doing good as well.

And, if we are to enter into his rest, it must be by entering into his beneficence, and by abiding in his holiness. Does it seem to us, as well it may, that of all words in human speech there is no sweeter word than this word, *rest?* Well, there is left to us a promise of entering into rest. Does it seem to us that all our human rest is transient, — for a season only, — ends presently in new and harder labors, — in renewed fatigue? Well, then, there is left to us a promise of entering into God's rest. He is never weary. He is never idle. We, too, shall be never weary. We, too, shall be never idle. We shall rest from sin. We shall rest in holiness. We shall rest in God. There, and only there, the wicked cease from troubling, and the weary are at rest.

Let us therefore fear, brethren, lest, a promise being left us of entering into his rest, any of us should seem to come short of it.

II.

THE PURPOSE OF THE JEWISH SABBATH.

"Keep the Sabbath day to sanctify it, as the Lord thy God hath commanded thee. Six days thou shalt labor, and do all thy work: But the seventh day is the Sabbath of the Lord thy God: in it thou shalt not do any work, thou, nor thy son, nor thy daughter, nor thy manservant, nor thy maidservant, nor thine ox, nor thine ass, nor any of thy cattle, nor thy stranger that is within thy gates; that thy manservant and thy maidservant may rest as well as thou. And remember that thou wast a servant in the land of Egypt, and that the Lord thy God brought thee out thence through a mighty hand and by a stretched out arm: therefore the Lord thy God commanded thee to keep the Sabbath day." — DEUT. v. 12-15.

IN the last sermon, we studied that sublime passage in the Book of Genesis which records the completion of God's creative work and the beginning of his rest. I tried to show that the divine rest from creation has continued ever since, and still continues; that the Sabbath of the Lord our God not only cometh, but now is. I tried to show also (so far as I might reverently touch upon such mysteries) wherein the rest of God consists, and how he is spending this long Sabbath day of his; that rest, to him, is not idleness nor inactivity, but rather a rising from the exercise of might and power to the still, strong exercise of his loving and eternal Spirit; and that he is spending his Sabbath in the sanctifying of the world, which, through six immemorial ages, he had been creating. And I reminded you of the gracious promise which is left to us, of entering into God's own rest; and tried to show how more than ever sweet and beautiful that promise sounds, when we discover that it is a rest of holiness, the rest of being good and doing good, the rest of tireless love.

This, then, the rest of God, is the true rest: this, the Sabbath of God, is the true Sabbath. We use words sometimes in a lower, sometimes in a higher, sense: we are obliged to use them so, partly because of the poverty of human speech, which has not words enough for every thing, and so compels some to do double duty; but more because of the relation of things seen to things unseen, and the correspondence between them. For example, we have only one word, "life," by which to designate the life of the body and the life of the soul: and we are obliged constantly to remind ourselves, that, when we use the word in its lower signification, we have not exhausted its meaning; that (as a favorite hymn-writer has expressed the thought), —

> "'Tis not the whole of life to live,
> Nor all of death to die;"

that the limited, temporal meaning of the word is but a shadow of its spiritual meaning. I know that the lower meaning is constantly absorbing our attention as if it were all. But it is not all. The true life, the real death, are of the soul, unseen, eternal.

So with this word "rest." We know what it means when we speak of bodily rest, of taking rest in sleep, of days of temporal rest. We know, that, even in this usage of the word, its meaning is very sweet and beautiful; that when we are worn out with weary labor, with work of toiling hands and busy feet and aching head, the comfort of repose is very great, nay, very necessary; that without it the unrefreshed body must become the victim of disease, the prey of death. We know that even every toiling beast must rest, or die. We know, by an experience which defines it better than all verbal definitions can, what rest is, and how comforting, how much to be desired, how not to be dispensed with, it is to every living creature.

But there is a higher rest, a nobler rest, a truer rest, than what is physical; just as there is a higher life, a nobler life, a truer life, than what is physical. As comforting and pleasant to the spirit as the repose of evening to the body, as much more blessed and complete and enduring as eternity is more perfect than time, is this true rest. It is that whereof the Lord Jesus spoke in words of gracious promise when he said, "Come unto me, all ye that labor and are heavy laden, and I will give you rest." It is that into which God has entered, and in which he now abides, his works being finished from the foundation of the world. It is that into which a promise is left us of entering also.

But of this rest it is not easy to conceive.

Eye hath not seen it. We have seen the body locked in the embrace of sleep, and watched its peaceful breathing when the labors of the day are over. But this spiritual rest is something which cannot be seen by mortal eyes. For the tired body, too, there are restful sounds that soothe the drowsy senses; there are refreshment and repose in pleasant music; or when we lie where branches sway and rustle over us, and the birds sing in them, there is rest in the very sounds which our ears hear. But this spiritual rest of which I speak, makes no such appeal to sense. Ear hath not heard it, neither has the imagination conceived it. It can only be known by being felt and enjoyed. Just as description of light is impossible to one born blind, so no definition, no description, no representation, of this spiritual rest is adequate for an unrestful soul. God must reveal it to us by his Spirit, if we are to know what it is. He must make us partakers of it. We must enter into it.

And this is what God is all the while inviting us to do, attracting us, impelling us to do; this is what he yearns to have us do; it is for this that all his government is exercised, that all his providence is arranged, that all his Spirit strives. And the way in which he leads us to this spiritual rest, as to all spiritual things, is through our natural experiences. First, that which is natural; then that which is spiritual. The lower first, and afterward the higher. That is the law. From things that are seen to things that are unseen. That is the order.

Remembering this, we begin to see the reason for the commandment which God gave the Hebrew people through his servant Moses, and which I have taken for a text. Here was a rude, self-willed, headstrong people, to be made quiet, religious, trustful, holy. This was the problem: a people to be trained and educated to a religious exaltation which should make them fit to be the religious teachers of the world; a race of more or less degraded slaves to be familiarized with spiritual truth, and purified by it. And this was the way the problem was solved: by a system of types and prophecies and shadows. Earth was made to them the hint of heaven. Nature was to lead them to the God of nature. Events of time and place were to suggest to them realities beyond time and superior to place. Things of sense were to be the media of things of spirit. The Jewish law cannot be understood, nor the worth and significance of it measured, unless this is constantly borne in mind.

For example, it was the design of the inspired leader of the Hebrew people, the great lawgiver and soldier who was God's instrument in making them a nation, — it was his design, or, let us rather say, it was God's design through him, to teach this people the great truth on which we have been meditating. It was no easy task. To make things unseen real and vivid; to lift their minds up to the truth of an immortal rest of peaceful holiness, when a host of busy cares, of snaring temptations, of hurtful passions, of degrading lusts, were dragging them downward, — this was a very difficult thing indeed. Persistent, patient, skilful schooling was necessary, as it is with an ignorant and perverse child. To use words in a lower sense at first, and gradually to lift them to their higher sense; to make use of the "illusiveness of life" (as Robertson beautifully calls it [1]), and to show what infinite stretch there is to truth, — how it draws out like an endless telescope; or how (to use another figure) it is a clew which, if you hold one end of it, you may follow out eternally, — this was the way, the only way, to do the work.

So the law of association was called in to teach the people. And as when men build a monument to mark some famous spot, or to commemorate some great achievement, or to perpetuate the memory of some illustrious life, that when the coming generations ask, "What is this monument?" the story of the place, or of the deed, or of the life, being associated with this material thing, this block of granite or of marble that can be touched and seen, may live, and not die: so Moses erected for this people a monumental day, that when, in the uniform succession of the days, it came around, and men should ask, "What is this day?" the higher truth attached to it should be permanent and powerful.

What, then, was this day? Moses called it

---

[1] Sermons by the late Rev. F. W. Robertson. Vol. iii. Sermon vi.

Sabbath,—which means rest. And so it was a Sabbath; not the real Sabbath, but a Sabbath, in some inferior meaning of the word. Not the real Sabbath, I say, for that, as we have seen, is constant and above time; not the perfect rest,—for that is uniform, perpetual, spiritual, —but, in some limited and lower meaning of the word, a rest; a Sabbath shadowy, imperfect, transient, that should yet, by its very imperfectness, suggest a real, enduring, perfect one. The idea of rest, the name of rest, was fastened on, declared to be sacred, emphasized with all the sanctions of religion. That of itself was a great thing. The result must be, that, after a while they would discover that no twenty-four hours' rest of body, merely, could exhaust the meaning of that sacred word, or meet the full requirements of that high idea.

But this was not all. The mysterious fact on which we pondered a week ago was linked inseparably to this day. It spoke of God's rest. The Hebrew people had a most imperfect notion, probably a gross, and often a wrong, notion of what God's rest is. But it was a great thing that the word could be connected anyhow with God. Already the idea of rest becomes immensely dignified and enlarged, by the mere fact that it belongs in any sense, however feebly understood, to him. And thus enlarged and dignified, it must sooner or later lift the people who receive it up above the world of sense, into the world of spirit.

But this was not all. This Jewish Sabbath had another association connected with it. When men asked, " What does this day mean ? " and " Why was it ordained ? " one answer would be the one on which we have just been meditating, " Because God rested." That is the reason given in the Book of Exodus. That was, probably enough, the religious truth which Abraham had handed down along the generations to the lawgiver Moses. But it is not probable that this fact was commemorated by what I have called a monumental day, until the exodus from Egypt. Probably Abraham knew that God had created, and that God had rested. But probably Abraham did not celebrate God's rest by a weekly Sabbath. There is only a very slender and unsatisfactory sum of evidence, only the very thinnest film of proof, to show that any weekly Sabbath was observed before the time of Moses.[1] But when, after the long years of slavery in Egypt, this oppressed and tired race of bondmen were emancipated; when the centuries of degrading toil were ended, and the tribes went forth, to look no more upon the hateful brick-yards where they and their fathers before them had worn out weary lives, and to hear no more the harsh voices of their cruel taskmasters; when, with new-formed hopes stirring within them, and the dawning consciousness of nationality dignifying them, they were marching toward a land which they might hope to call their own, a goodly land, a land of hills and valleys, a land of milk and honey, — then there was ordained this Sabbath day, which should always speak to them and to the generations

[1] Probably the best summary of the argument on this point is to be found in Hessey's Bampton Lectures (1860), to which volume, and to the authorities copiously quoted therein, it is sufficient to refer any readers who may desire to inform themselves concerning it. Quotations are given in still greater detail (especially from theologians since the Reformation) in Cox's Literature on the Sabbath Question, — a book of marvellous learning and research. But the narration in this sixteenth chapter of Exodus speaks for itself so clearly that it scarcely needs much comment.

after them, of slavery and rest from slavery, of toil and rest from toil, of degradation and deliverance from degradation, of sorrow changed to joy, of trouble ending in exceeding blessedness.

Thus it was, and then it was, that this seventh-day Sabbath was instituted. It was in the wilderness. I read the story of it in the chapter from the Book of Exodus this morning (chap. xvi.). The people had come out of Egypt exultant and rejoicing that their toil was over; there was no more work for them thenceforth, they thought; they were free at last from the weary servitude of centuries. It is easy to conceive the gratulation which inspired them as they thought of this; it is easy to conceive what present meaning this word "rest" would have for them, and how it would seem of all words the sweetest. But they had not been long started on their journey before they found that they were very far from being yet at rest. As soon as they were fairly in the wilderness, and the enthusiasm of their deliverance was over, and the hardships of the journey through the desert began to make themselves felt the began to grumble and despond, and to say that this was worse than Egypt, and to wish that they were back again. They had not found the rest they thought they had. Want and hunger and toilsome journeying had come upon them instead. And they murmured against their leaders.

Something had to be done now, to meet the exigency, and to teach this fickle, ignorant, childish people patience and faith. So God sent the quails and the manna, and they were fed; but with this provision of necessary food came also, by inspired wisdom, the ordinance of the Sabbath day. When the sixth day came, they were to gather food for two days, and to rest upon the seventh. On the seventh day, if they went out to look for manna, as some disorderly persons did, they could not find it, because there was none to find. This seventh day was to speak to them of rest, was to be a constant prophecy of rest, to cheer their discontented spirits, to encourage their distrustful hearts. It was to say to them, so often as it came, "The promise which was given to you of entering into rest shall not be unfulfilled. A rest remains for you. You have come out of Egypt forever; and though you are in the wilderness still, and have hardships and discomforts and fatigues to endure, plenty of them, do not be discouraged: there is verily a rest in store, surely a rest remains. Take heart, and trust in God for it." This was what the seventh day declared to them so often as it came.

Naturally enough, they at first supposed this promise was to be fulfilled as soon as they should get out of the wilderness. They used to say to themselves, probably, while they were wandering through those perilous deserts, "This is hard, but let us wait until we enter Canaan: it will all be over then. Then we shall be at rest. That is a goodly land, beautiful, well watered, rich and bountiful, and, more than all, our own. Wait till we get there. It will all be over then. And then we shall be at rest."

So, after forty years of toilsome wandering, and after one whole generation of the people had been worn out in the desert, the long-looked-for day arrived. They crossed the boundary river, and they entered into the goodly land. It was indeed a goodly land, but it was not a land of rest to them. Beset by foes on every hand, compelled to fight for standing-ground with enemies not few nor feeble, they had but a stormy and unrestful time of it. And presently the truth began to dawn on them, that Joshua, their new leader, had not given them rest any more than Moses had; that the rest, the true rest, the rest which their souls needed, was not to be had even here, was not, at least, to be had yet. But all the time this seventh day kept coming, with its significant name, with its clustering associations, with its mysterious reference to the rest of God, with its historic connection with their deliverance from bondage. Surely this must mean something. They had not found its meaning yet, but they could not help believing that it had a meaning. So the Sabbath day remained a constant and illusive prophecy.

And so the years rolled by, and still continual wars harassed them; and if for a little time there came a season of prosperity, it was broken up again by some calamity: just as, though the Sabbath came at intervals of seven days, to bring repose to tired bodies and to toiling hands, to master and to servant and to cattle, yet it was soon over, and the weary round of work-day labor, and of fighting, and of troubles, would begin again. Until in David's time (or a little later), the "rest" was seen to be still future, and more remote and vague than ever; and they had ceased to look for it so confidently as temporal and earthly. Still the seventh day returned and kept returning; but, to the more thoughtful and spiritually minded of the people, it was now prophetic of things higher, things unseen, things scarcely to be defined in speech. That sublime call to worship in the ninety-fifth Psalm indicates this growth and discipline of the people, and their exaltation to a higher stand-point. "Let us worship and fall down," the Psalmist says, "let us bow before the Lord our Maker." He created us. He is leading us. He has rest in store for us. What it is we know not. Many have failed of it. But it still remains. I think the very structure of this Psalm is full of eloquent suggestion. It begins with a burst of worshipful acclamation; but it sinks to silent reverence and awe, and closes in a hush of mingled fear and hope on that word "rest,"—as if the meaning of it could not perfectly be uttered.

So this thought of rest kept growing stronger, even although it was growing higher and seemingly more distant. It was a thought which never lost its hold upon the people. It was the central thought of their religious system. Six days they might forget it, but on the seventh they remembered it. The idea was so wedged into their religious observances that it could not possibly be taken out without the dislocation of them all. The weekly Sabbath was not the only Sabbath. There was a Sabbath of weeks as well as of days; and a Sabbath of months; and a great, memorable, wonderful Sabbath of years,—of rest for a whole year, every fiftieth year.[1] The Sabbath of days pointed to the Sabbath of weeks, and this again to the Sabbath of months, and this again to the Sabbath of years, and this—to what? Could it be that the mind of the Hebrew peo-

[1] Exod. xxiii. 10–13: cf. especially Lev. xxiii. 3, 15, 24, 33–39; xxv. 1–24; xxvi. 2; Deut. xv.

ple, led on and up, thus far, would stop here? Would it not almost of necessity rise higher yet, — even from earth to heaven? Or let me put the case a little differently. The seventh day in its weekly return reminded them of rest from slavery, of rescue from Egypt, of repose in Canaan. But this, — had this no higher meaning? was this all? Was there not a better Canaan, a happier land, a repose more perfect, where no foes could enter, where no evils could annoy, where no sorrows could trouble, where no death could kill? And then would come the thought — there must be such a rest, for we are told that God rested; and surely his rest can be no fitful, transient, troubled rest, like ours.

It will not be possible, within the limits of one sermon, to finish our examination of the Hebrew Sabbath. Already it is evident that there is much to be learned from a wise study of it. All that I have tried to do, to-day, is to set forth the purpose of that Sabbath, and the meaning of it. And for that reason I took for my text, not the commandment as it is written in Exodus, but the commandment as it is written in Deuteronomy. The reason for the Jewish Sabbath which is given in Exodus, is the rest of God. The reason for it given in the Book of Deuteronomy, is the rest in Canaan. But from both books it is evident that the seventh-day Sabbath was not ordained for its own sake merely, but for some other and higher reason. It was a day of prophecy. It was a day of promise. Week after week it came to this Hebrew people, and found them sinful, toilsome, tired still. Generation after generation they lived in Canaan; and this day returning found them troubled, restless, sinful still. Centuries of hard experience taught them more and more perfectly the bitter lesson which found expression, at last, in the words of one of their own prophets, that the "wicked are like the troubled sea, which cannot rest." They could not rest. They were not at peace with God. Their kings and soldiers and legislators — David, Joshua, Moses — had not given them rest, could not give them rest. And yet here the day was, coming, coming, in its regular return, and coming only to be a mockery, a bitter mockery, unless there was a real rest remaining. So they clung to the persuasion that there was such a rest. And at last the son of David came, another Joshua, a prophet greater than Moses, bringing grace and truth and life, and rest eternal. Then the significance of all these monumental days and rites and ceremonies became apparent.

Of course, then, the seventh day was not the Sabbath, is not the Sabbath. The Sabbath is not a day of twenty-four hours at all. The seventh day may be a Sabbath; or the first day may be a Sabbath, if there is any reason for making it so, as we shall by and by find there is a most sufficient reason; any day may be a Sabbath, as John Calvin, at the time of the Reformation, seems to have proposed, most unwisely, to make Thursday a Sabbath;[1] or, better still, every day of Christian life may be a Sabbath, — the type and prophecy, nay, more, the earnest and foretaste of the eternal rest. If the Sabbath of God be a mere twenty-four hours' rest, then it must be the seventh day; and I do not see how any logic can escape the obligation to acknowledge it, or bridge the

[1] Cf. Hessey, p. 142, and Cox. vol. 2, p. 121.

insuperable chasm which, on that theory, separates the seventh day from the first, and from all others. But if the Sabbath be eternal in the heavens, and all days of time but shadowy types of that eternal day, then, whether it may be the seventh day that men commemorate, or the first day, or any day, or every day, can make no fatal difference.

Nor is this all. The story of the wandering of these Hebrew tribes is not without its present and most practical significance to us, — the story of their wanderings and of their disappointments, and of their illusive types and shadows. "These things" said an apostle,[1] "were our examples; . . . and they are written for our admonition, upon whom the ends of the world are come." Have we not also wandered in deserts and in wildernesses, restless and unsatisfied? Have not we been seeking rest in God's creatures, and not in God himself? Have we not tried to be content with shadows rather than with the eternal substance of the Sabbath? And have we not learned — some of us, I am sure, have learned

---

[1] 1 Cor. x. 1-11.

at last — that there is rest for us only in God? We have learned, at last, to say with St. Augustine, "Thou hast made us for thyself, and our heart is restless till it rest in thee."[1] Let us remember, then, that earth cannot furnish us the perfect Sabbath, — that time does not contain it. It is the rest of God. It is eternal in the heavens.

This is the practical and important lesson with which I suspend this meditation. And to sum up and enforce what I have been trying to say, I borrow these stanzas, antique and quaint, but very beautiful and very true, from good George Herbert. The lesson which was taught the Hebrew people in their weekly Sabbath, the lesson which we need to learn by all our personal human experiences, is the lesson which this poem also teaches, in language better than I can find : —

>"When God at first made man,
>Having a glasse of blessings standing by,
>Let us (said he) poure on him all we can :
>Let the world's riches, which dispersèd lie,
>   Contract into a span.

[1] Confessions, i. 1.

So strength first made a way;
Then beautie flow'd; then wisdome, honor, pleasure:
When almost all was out, God made a stay,
Perceiving that alone, of all his treasure,
　　Rest in the bottome lay.

　　For, if I should (said he)
Bestow this jewell also on my creature,
He would adore my gifts instead of me,
And rest in nature, not the God of nature:
　　So both should losers be.

　　Yet let him keep the rest,
But keep them with repining restlessnesse:
Let him be rich and wearie, that at least,
If goodnesse leade him not, yet wearinesse
　　May tosse him to my breast."

III.

THE USE AND ABUSE OF THE JEWISH SABBATH.

"Therefore said some of the Pharisees, This man is not of God, because he keepeth not the Sabbath day." — JOHN ix. 16.

WHAT, then, had this man done by which the Sabbath day was violated? And who was he who was proved thus to be "not of God"?

The story is familiar to us all. It was Jesus of Nazareth, the young prophet of Galilee, concerning whom some men had already begun to believe that he was the Messiah. It was now more than two years since he had begun his public ministry as a religious teacher; and during all this time he had been conspicuous among men for words of singular wisdom, for deeds of very beautiful and tender compassion, and of wonderful power, — in a word, for a life spent in doing good. No one could lay to his charge an unkind, dishonorable, or selfish act. No one could accuse him of immorality, or of any violation of the law of love. He had enemies, to be sure, plenty of them — bitter ones; enemies quick to detect iniquity in him, had there been iniquity; enemies who were conspiring against him, and, on one pretext or another, continually denouncing him as untrustworthy and bad. They could not charge him with violating any moral law, but they could charge him with neglect of traditional ceremonies. They could not deny that he healed sick men; but they could insist that he healed them in some irregular way, or by some malign power. If they were obliged to confess, sometimes, that he had done good, at least they could criticise his methods, and condemn, as evil, the place, the time, or some attendant circumstance. It is always instructive to know what a man's enemies say of him. And when they can find no charge to produce, except a quibble or a technicality, when they can say nothing against the spirit of a man, but only something against his forms, — such as a violation of usage or tradition or ceremonial rite, — the fact is most significant.

Such an instance was the one referred to in the text. Jesus, passing along through the streets of Jerusalem, had seen an unfortunate man who had been blind from his birth. Besides the calamity of blindness, there attached to him also some stigma of moral disgrace, as if his blindness must be the result of special and pre-eminent sinfulness, either on his own part or on the part of his parents, — so that the man was made out to be, not merely unfortunate, but infamous. We need not pursue the story, except to say that Jesus rejected peremptorily the notion that the man's blindness was the mark of any conspicuous sinfulness; and then, by an act of gracious power, removed the life-long darkness by which he had been afflicted, doing thus a double service to the unhappy man, and sending him away thankful and astonished.

Certainly this was a kind and gracious thing to do: and certainly, the wisdom which Christ had shown in his exposure of the cruel notion held by his disciples, and by the community at large; the power which he had shown in the miracle of healing; the love which he had shown in his treatment of the sufferer, — all these might have secured the approval of the Pharisees, and might have seemed to them, sitting as the religious authorities of the nation, like credentials of a divine mission on the part of Jesus. But, as it happened, the day on which this deed had been performed, was the weekly Sabbath, on which, according to the commandment, there must be no work performed. To open the eyes of the blind was work, — thus they argued; and even our Lord himself seemed to admit it, — for when he did the miracle, it was with the solemn words, "I must work the works of him that sent me, while it is day." So, then, this was work: but the commandment forbids work on the Sabbath; but this was on the Sabbath; therefore Jesus has not kept God's commandment; therefore he cannot be of God, — and being not of God, no further hint was needful to indicate whence, in their opinion, he must be. All the wisdom of his words, all the power and skill of his deed, all the loving and pure compassion of his spirit, was to pass for nothing, because he did not keep the Sabbath day! Or, rather let us say, because he did not keep it as they thought it should be kept; because his opinions did not square with theirs; because his manners were not strict enough, according to their standard.

I wish to take this story as giving us a glimpse of how the Jewish Sabbath was regarded in the time of Christ, and of the strict and literal exactness with which the command to keep it holy was observed; an exactness so strict and literal, that it might even make the day unholy, irksome, evil. Remember that the Pharisees were the religious teachers of the people, sitting, as our Lord said, in Moses' seat, and looked up to as the recognized and authoritative expounders of the law. Remember also that this was not the only instance when they found fault with Jesus as a Sabbath-breaker. Over and over again this charge was brought, and in such a way as indicates that they were very much in earnest in it, and even believed themselves to be in the right in making it. On the other hand, our Lord himself seems to have been in no way careful to avoid giving occasion for the charge, even taking pains sometimes to do things publicly upon the Sabbath day which he knew might be complained of and brought up against him. And his reply to the Pharisees, when they made the charge, was, not that he was justified in violating the Sabbath, but that he had not violated the Sabbath. He acknowledged that he was still a Jew, and that it was becoming in him to fulfil all righteousness. So he was circumcised. So he was baptized by John. So he offered sacrifice and observed festivals. So he conformed to the law of Moses; and, as I say, the way in which he defended himself, the ground which he took in reply to this accusation, was, that he had not broken the Sabbath, but had kept it.

Which was right, — he, or they? Was the Jewish Sabbath what they made it, or was it what he made it? And, if they were wrong, wherein did their mistake consist?

We cannot hesitate, of course, in our answer to the first question. And the answer to the first involves the answer to the second. The Jewish Sabbath was meant to be a privilege. The Pharisees had made it a bondage. It was meant to be a holy day. But the Pharisees, by such interpretation of its holiness as they would have enforced on Jesus, made it an unholy day; so that, though upon six days it might be lawful to do good, upon the seventh to do good was not lawful, and such an act as the opening a blind man's eyes became wicked. The Sabbath was meant to be a means. They would make it an end of itself. God designed it as a sign of something higher. They treated it as if it were itself the thing signified. As I said a week ago, it was a Sabbath, but not the perfect, the real Sabbath. The trouble with them was, that they treated it as if it were the real and perfect Sabbath. They are not the only ones who have fallen into this error, and have rested in the letter rather than in the spirit; have been content with the body rather than with the soul of things; have grasped at the shadow and let go the substance; have stopped short with things seen and temporal, and not looked at the things which are unseen and eternal.

This was the difference between Christ and the Pharisees. Christ's reverence for the law of Moses was not less than theirs, it was unspeakably greater. He did not come to destroy it, he came to fulfil it. He saw, and he aimed to show, that the spirit of that law was greater than the letter of it could hold, and must, presently, throw off the letter as a husk, and hinderance of its greatness. Guide-posts are good while one is journeying, but he does not need them when he has reached his journey's end. Hope is good, till one has the fruition of the thing hoped for; and then it ceases to be necessary. So the Jewish types and prophecies were good, until the realities of which they spoke arrived, and then they were no longer useful. The time was close at hand when all these should pass away,— close at hand, but not yet quite present. Men were Jews yet. Even our Lord himself was a Jew, observing the Jewish law. He was in the flesh as yet. And though he was himself the truth to which all these types and monuments and ordinances pointed, yet the veil, that is to say, his flesh, hid him for the present. In a little while he would be lifted up; the veil, that is to say, his flesh, would be laid aside; he would be present in the Spirit, nearer, everywhere, always,— and then the ordinances were to cease. But as yet they were to be observed, and he himself set the example of perfect observance.

One of these types and ordinances was the seventh-day Sabbath. Presently that was to cease. But it had not ceased as yet. It was a good thing, a useful type, a pleasant promise, a most serviceable means. It was made for man. And the true way to reverence it was to use it as a privilege, to employ it as a means. Without doubt Jesus rested on the seventh day, and was glad enough to rest. Without doubt, when the six days were over, with their trials in the carpenter's shop, or with their weary round of journeyings from village to village, with their thronging multitudes claiming his care and time and painful anxiety, — without doubt this seventh day was a blessed day to the fatigued and tired teacher and his twelve friends and followers. No doubt the privileges of the synagogue, with its worship, public and formal, of the God of Israel, were welcome. No doubt he rested from his weekly duties and employments, counting it a privilege and even a duty so to rest. But if the Pharisees attempted to compel him to the observance of their foolish and unscriptural strictnesses: to say that, if he saw a blind man whom he could give sight to, he must let him stay blind; if he saw a sick man, that he must not heal him; if he passed hungry through the corn-fields, that he must not pluck, in passing, a few ears to eat, because all this was work, — then he would say, that the Pharisees were trying to make the commandment of God of none effect by their traditions, and were abusing the Sabbath instead of using it.

It is probable that we have, even at this day, a mistaken impression concerning the Jewish Sabbath. From the repeated emphasis which is put upon the observance of it in the Hebrew Scriptures; from the penalties which, by the Jewish law, were threatened and sometimes enforced upon the violation of it; from a false idea of what keeping a thing holy means, and of wherein holiness consists, — from these and other causes we have accustomed ourselves to believe that it was an irksome day, a sad and gloomy day, a fast, a day on which to afflict one's soul. It was not such a day. To make it such a day was to abuse it. If it was defended by penalties, it was for the same reason that a perverse child is prevented by penalties from over-exerting himself in any way, or from running into any kind of danger. To read of a man stoned for gathering sticks on the Sabbath may startle us at first, and may make it look as if the day were a harsh and severe institution. But it was because the day was so beneficent that the crime of a man who undertook to destroy it was so heinous. Moses was very much in earnest, had to be very much in earnest; and he was not willing that an institution, which was given to be a blessing to the nation, through generation after generation, should be destroyed at the very outset by one rebellious and mischievous man. So he had him put to death,[1] and made of him a conspicuous example that was remembered through all coming time, so long as the Jews were a nation. But we make a great mistake if we sup-

---

[1] Num. xv. 32–36. It is to be observed that this, the only recorded instance of the infliction of the death-penalty for Sabbath breaking, occurred "while the children of Israel were in the wilderness," — when the Sabbath was as yet a new thing, and the value of it needed to be signally emphasized.

pose, that because the penalties which guarded and preserved the day were severe, therefore the day itself was severe. The one only commandment concerning it was, that it should be a rest-day. No possible language could have conveyed to that nation of emancipated slaves a gladder idea of it than that it was a day on which they need not work. They knew what work was, with a very sorrowful knowledge, indeed; but, for centuries, they had hardly known what rest was. And an ordinance which ordained for them a seventh part of their whole time, during which they need not work, but might sleep, and recreate and enjoy themselves, with the assurance that in so doing they were doing nothing wrong, but were even performing a sacred duty, with the knowledge that they were pleasing God by thus being happy, — this was a privilege so beneficent, a boon so gracious, that, when fairly understood, it could not fail to be a very welcome and most precious ordinance.

If it seems to some that the injunction against work must have made the day a fast-day, it may be worth-while to say a word or two upon that point. They could not, it is true, cook on the Sabbath day; but to a rude and simple people that was no great deprivation. They could eat, and they could even feast.[1] Social visiting was not forbidden, nor the giving of a feast, provided the feast involved no labor on the part of master or of servant in the household. In the statement of the law of the Sabbath given in Deuteronomy, the reason why there could be no cooking appears, — "that thy man-servant and thy maid-servant may rest as well as thou." It was not at all that the day should thus be made a fast-day. And it must be remembered, that in those early times, and among that rude and simple people, cooking had not become a fine art; and it was thought possible to exist and even to be happy upon very simple fare. Whether the change which has taken place

---

[1] The incident recorded in Luke xiv. 1-24, especially v. 7, indicating that the feast was on a somewhat large scale, is sufficiently decisive on this point. But see also Alford's note on this passage, and Trench on the parable of "The Great Supper;" also the authorities quoted by Cox, under the article "Feasting on the Sabbath;" also the article "Sabbath," in Smith's Dictionary of the Bible; also the noteworthy article on "The Talmud," in the London Quarterly Review for October, 1867, Am. ed., p. 232.

since then, and the difference between our usages and tastes and theirs, is wholly an advance, it is foreign to the scope of this discourse to discuss.

What I am insisting on is, that the seventh-day rest which Moses enjoined upon the Jewish people was designed to be a blessing and not a bondage. It was to be a symbol of a greater blessing in store for them, but it was also to be itself a blessing. It could scarcely speak to them of happiness hereafter, if it were not itself happy. It was to be made holy; but holiness did not mean austerity nor acerbity nor asceticism. It was to be a pure day, a clean day, or, as the word translated "holy" may suggest by its derivation,[1] a bright day; if you please, a shining or sunny day. Its cheerfulness was to prophesy the cheerfulness of heaven. Its social enjoyments were to suggest the fellowship of heaven. To be happy on this day was a privilege, nay, was even a duty. And you cannot find in all the law of Moses any thing that even looks like making

---

[1] See Gesenius' Lexicon, s. v. קרש, and the perhaps kindred הרש, of which the primary idea is "to be bright."

it a hardship. Was it any hardship to that people, aching in all their bones with their centuries of unpaid toil, to be told that they might rest?[1] We know how a slave feels when he is told that he may have a holiday. We know how a school-boy feels when he is told that he may have a recess. To tell him that he must not study till the recess is over, to even impose a penalty upon him for doing so, is no such very dreadful thing.

Unquestionably, the seventh-day Sabbath began to lose something of its original character, long before the time of the gospel history. Studying the Old Testament, we discover on the one hand a growing formality, on the other hand a growing superstition. It was characteristic of that Hebrew people, it is characteristic of all peoples more or less, to run from one extreme to another. After they came to be settled in their own land, and had begun to

[1] A striking illustration of this is to be found in a fact related by an observant traveller concerning the slaves in the Southern States. No hymn sung in their religious meetings was more popular than "Welcome, sweet day of rest." At a Sunday-morning prayer-meeting it would sometimes be sung three or four times over in the course of the hour.

feel the pride of prosperity, and to forget the hardships of their Egyptian slavery, it was not pleasant to be reminded all the time of that degrading fact. When a man gets to be rich, he does not like to be reminded that he was once poor. When a man has achieved distinction of any sort, he will not thank you to tell him that he or his father was once a very humble and ordinary man. It hurts his pride. So with this people. They were not very fond of remembering that they were servants in the land of Egypt. But this was what their seventh-day Sabbath was designed to remind them of, through all generations. So it became convenient to them, presently, to fix their attention upon the day, rather than upon what it commemorated. So, too, when they were engrossed with earthly things, had waxed fat and sordid, and had learned the vices of prosperity, it was not pleasant to have this seventh day come pricking in upon their luxury and sloth and sensuality, and reminding them that here was not their rest, — that their true rest was beyond, that their real rest was above. So, for this reason also, it was convenient to fix their attention on the day itself, and not on what it prophesied. The day was meant to point backward, and to point forward. But it was not pleasant for this ungrateful and sordid people to look either way. Backward was Egypt, and the disgrace of slavery. Forward was — who cared for what was forward? " Let us eat and drink and be merry," here and now : we need no other rest !

So, easily enough, naturally enough, the day came to be, either a merely formal thing, or else a dreadfully superstitious thing. It had come to be a mere form in the time of the prophet Isaiah. The people had ignored its meaning; and, though they kept up the show of its observance, they considered it a bore, and they made of it a mockery. So that God is represented as saying to them at the beginning of Isaiah's prophecy,[1] in indignant and sorrowful reproof, " Bring no more vain oblations ; . . . the new moons and Sabbaths . . . I cannot away with. . . . Your new moons and your appointed feasts my soul hateth." Their religious observances, of which the Sabbath was

[1] Chap. i. 13, 14.

the central and most conspicuous institution, had come to be a mere form. They meant nothing, expressed nothing, suggested nothing. The soul had gone out of them; and, though the body remained, it was a dry and dead body. The Sabbath was no longer "a delight, — the holy of the Lord, and honorable."

A still more perfect picture of this merely formal observance of the Jewish Sabbath is suggested by a passage in the book of the prophet Amos. This prophet was a contemporary of Isaiah; and his exhortations to the nation are prompted by the same circumstances, the same sins, the same errors, which give point to the prophecies of Isaiah. The selfish and corrupt people are described (chap. viii. 5, 6) as fretting beneath the Sabbath rest, as if it were a yoke imposed upon them, and as having turned what was a privilege into a meaningless and irksome formality. "When will the new moon be gone," they say, "that we may sell corn? and the Sabbath that we may set forth wheat, making the ephah small and the shekel great" (giving scant measure and charging a large price), "and falsifying the balances by deceit?"

Here, even in a more striking form than in the passages before quoted, is the picture of a Sabbath which had lost all significance, which commemorated nothing, which pointed forward to nothing, which was without value or charm; a monument from which the inscription had been obliterated; a guide-post which pointed no way. Cherished for itself alone,—when it was cherished at all,—it had become distasteful to men and a mockery to God.

Well, the result of this religious declension, of which the contempt of the Sabbath was the most conspicuous instance, was disaster and captivity to the nation. Since they had learned to hold the thought of rest so cheap, they should be sent to school again to learn the value of it. Captivity in Egypt had made it very welcome once; perhaps captivity in Assyria might make it very welcome again. And so there came upon the Jews that period of exile and disgrace, seventy years of sorrow and humiliation and hardship.[1] When they came back again into their own land, they began to observe the Sabbath with renewed zeal. Stricter

[1] 2 Chron. xxxvi. 21.

and more detailed regulations for its observance were enjoined by Nehemiah.[1] But the significance of the day as a religious privilege was never quite regained. And presently the observance of it, enforced thus by the strong arm of the law, began to degenerate into superstition. The headstrong nation had not learned its lesson yet. They had learned that to give up their Sabbath was not safe. But they had not learned that their Sabbath was a blessing, and not a bondage. So they kept the day, but they kept it under terror. They began to invent new laws concerning it. The comprehensive law of Moses, which insisted simply and broadly, that on this day every one should have the right to rest, was thought to be insufficient. Stricter and stricter were the lines of obligation drawn, till, a little while before the time of our Saviour, during the progress of the Maccabean wars, a thousand Jews, brave but mistaken men, were slain without resistance on the Sabbath day, because the superstitious rigor which had grown up since the captivity made them think it unlawful to defend themselves.[2]

[1] Neh. x. 31; xiii. 15, 22.
[2] 1 Macc. ii. 38; and Josephus' Antiquities, B. xii., ch. vi. 2.

Such a thing could scarcely have occurred in the time of Moses. It was a rigorous observance of the letter, and the letter killed.

This incident, indeed, gave to the superstitious notion concerning the Sabbath a great shock; but it did not cure it. The scribes and Pharisees kept binding burdens heavier and heavier all the time, till, in the time of our Lord, they were most grievous to be borne. One school of zealots even taught, that, in whatever posture the Sabbath day should overtake a man, in that posture he must remain till the day was over; if standing when the sun set on Friday evening, then let him stand till Saturday at evening; if sitting, let him sit still, because to rise was to work. I might multiply instances, some of them so trivial that they would be even unfit to mention, of this same literalism, of this superstitious bondage to the seventh day.

I do not say that all these notions were current among the Pharisees and indorsed by them, but they are extreme examples of what was the prevalent Pharisaic error. To open the eyes of a blind man on the Sabbath day, was a crime so great that the goodness of the deed must pass for nothing, — this was the position which they held. The day was positively made unholy, by being reverenced for itself and not for what it signified. They made an idol of it. They acted as if this day of twenty-four hours was what men were made for, and as if they should expend their energies in its observance.

I have drawn out this history at a good deal of length, to show wherein the mistake of the Pharisees consisted. They had not used the Sabbath, they had suffered it to use them. They had swerved from the Mosaic commandment, by making the sign conspicuous, and losing sight of the thing signified. Kept for itself, as a dry ordinance, it was worse than useless. It did not turn their thoughts backward along the way through which the Lord their God had led them; nor did it turn their thoughts forward, telescopically opening up eternity before them. It was an institution to be microscopically scrutinized, to be given to God because he had arbitrarily demanded it, to be literally kept, although the letter might be irksome, cruel, deadly.

It was not so to Jesus. He appealed from the Pharisees to Moses, from the letter to the spirit. He showed how the Sabbath was a means, and not an end; was to be observed as a privilege, and as a prophecy of the eternal Sabbath, and not to be worn as a yoke of bondage, bowing men's faces down to earth instead of raising them to heaven. Such a privilege and prophecy it was to him. How he must have prized its welcome rest, when, footsore, weary, burdened, almost broken-hearted with the heavy load of human griefs and sicknesses which he had taken on himself to carry, and with no time that he could call his own, this day would come with opportunities for quiet, for retirement, for religious worship in the synagogue, or on the mountains, or in whatever solitudes might be found, and for fellowship with the few friends who loved and trusted him! And what wonderful and pathetic sacredness of meaning must the day have had to him, — speaking to him, as it did, of that other Jesus, who, centuries before, had led his people over Jordan into Canaan, but had not been able, after all, to give them rest, — speaking to him also of the rest from sin into which he himself had come to gather them!

Brethren, this Jewish Sabbath is a thing of the past. It was a prophecy, a type, a shadow. It is, as I shall presently show, no longer binding. But if we think there are no lessons to be taught us by the history of it, we shall strangely err. For the mistake of the Pharisees has been reproduced in Christian times. Their one great error was in taking shadow for substance; in supposing the Sabbath to be nothing but a twenty-four hours' day, not seeing that the real Sabbath is eternal in the heavens. Perhaps we have made a similar mistake. They thought it was the seventh day. Perhaps we think it is the first day. But it is not the first. It was not the seventh. The seventh was a type of it. The first may be a promise of it. But the real rest is unseen, spiritual, eternal.

And this general mistake of theirs included, as we have seen, two subordinate errors. This first: thinking that it was an earthly day merely, they made it sometimes a formality, and sometimes a superstition. First they neglected it and violated it. Then they were afraid of it and worshipped it.

And this secondly: regarding it in such a narrow, literal way, they came to think that they were made for it, not it for them; that God had, of his arbitrary will, enjoined it, not for their use and interest, but for his own; and that their obligation to observe it was a duty which they owed to him, and not a privilege conferred upon themselves. Christ, by his right use of the day, exposed this error. He showed them that their interest and God's interest were not antagonistic, were not separate and twain, but one. God's rest was their rest. They were to keep the day to him, because he had given it to them. They were not made for it, but it for them.[1]

This was the true idea of the Jewish Sabbath. It has seemed necessary to draw out this idea, and to distinguish the right observance of the day from the abuse of it, in order that we may be ready for the intelligent appreciation of our weekly Christian festival. For the Lord's Day is the heir of the Jewish Sabbath. It has displaced it throughout the Chris-

---

[1] Dr. Hessey's comment on this important verse (Mark ii. 27) is interesting and forcible. (See Hessey, p. 123.)

tian world. It has inherited its memories and its hopes. It has been treated with the same abuses, and marked by the same errors. To the consideration of this Christian festival we must next address ourselves.

IV.

THE LORD'S DAY A PRIVILEGE.

"And upon the first day of the week, when the disciples came together to break bread, Paul preached unto them, ready to depart on the morrow; and continued his speech until midnight." — ACTS xx. 7.

IT is from such slight hints as that afforded by this text, that we get what imperfect knowledge we possess concerning the life and usages of the early Christians. The life of Christ himself upon the earth is only partially reported: although, being reported by four different biographers, we get glimpses of it from four different points of view; and so the record gives forth more light, as a diamond does when it is cut with facets. But, when we know so little of the life of the Master, it is no wonder that we know less of the life of his disciples. Concerning these first pillars in the Christian church, and concerning the great work which was given them to do, — the work of moulding the institutions of Christianity, and defining and constructing its theology, — the authoritative record is very incomplete. The book of the Acts of the Apostles, and the hints in the various letters of the apostles, are the only inspired sources of information; and even from these the knowledge on these points has to be carefully and laboriously dug out, like precious metal from a bed of ore. Precisely how the first Christian churches were organized, for example; precisely what was their doctrinal belief; precisely what were their religious usages and ordinances, — these are questions which it is not easy authoritatively to answer. "How was baptism administered?" is a question which divides the church with a singular and almost hopeless bitterness of division, even at the present day. But if we search the New Testament for explicit directions to baptize in this or that way, and in none other, we cannot find them. Some people wonder at this. "How much trouble might have been saved to the church," they say, "what wrangling, what breaches of Christian charity, what scandal, what disunion, might have been prevented, if in some one of the Gospels, or in some one of Paul's epistles, there had been ten words of positive commandment on this subject!" But, search the whole New Testament as we may, those ten words of positive commandment cannot be found.

These are illustrations and examples of one general fact which needs to be constantly borne in mind, and which may be stated as follows: The kingdom of heaven which our Lord Jesus Christ established on the earth, and of which he himself is the eternal King, is an invisible and spiritual kingdom. It is within men. And its force and operation is from within, outward. It makes its appearance on the earth unarmed, unfurnished with worldly resources. It brings with it no laws written on stone tables, or on parchment rolls, or on paper pages. It establishes no courts to minister its justice. It erects no throne, and provides no sceptre for the sway of its submissive subjects. It is not meat nor drink. It is not circumcision nor uncircumcision. It is not observance of rites and ordinances, nor is it non-observance of rites and ordinances. It may use them, or it may refuse them. It is spiritual. Righteousness, peace, joy in the Holy Ghost, — this is the kingdom. Love, — this is the essence of it. Trust, — this is the condition and commencement of it. What Christ brought from heaven to earth was not an institution nor a cluster of institutions; not a law nor a code of laws; nor a form, nor a set of forms; but a spirit, a living spirit, a divine spirit, even the Holy Spirit, the eternal Helper and Sanctifier, to dwell in men, moulding them, strengthening them, giving them life, making them, and, through them, making all things new!

Therefore, when our Lord finished the work which he had to do in his flesh, and ascended into heaven, he left after him no organized church, and, I had almost said, no instituted ordinances. Baptism, indeed (which was already practised in the Jewish church), he sanctioned as a fit and useful, and even, commonly, a necessary symbol of discipleship. And the Lord's Supper, too, he instituted as at once a symbol and a means of the communion of his saints with him, and one with another. But these two exceptions are so simple as scarcely to do more than confirm the rule. He left no churches on the earth. He left disciples, and committed to them the organization of churches, — to them, guided and inspired by the Spirit of wisdom and of love. Questions of order, matters of detail, habits of worship and of Christian living, these were all things of Christian expediency, which needed not to be ordained beforehand. The living Spirit was to construct its body, fashioning it in strength and beauty, and in constant growth of perfectness.

To declare, then, as it seems to me we must honestly declare, that we can find no commandment in the New Testament, nor indeed in the whole Bible, requiring the observance of a weekly Sabbath on the part of Christians, need not surprise anybody. You can find no commandment requiring the organization of churches after a given form; no pattern shown, as there was to Moses in the mount, after which the institutions of the church must be constructed. You cannot find any catalogue of maxims covering cases of conscience, obedience to which is a test of discipleship. Nay, more. You do find the first inspired teachers of the church expressly disavowing the right of anybody to impose such maxims and regulations upon the church, to require the observance of feasts or fasts, to compel or to forbid any outward observance. So that we may even say, that if there were found in the New Testament any text explicitly requiring the observance of the first day of the week, for example, as a holy day, that text would be in such manifest and glaring contrast with the whole spirit of the remaining contents of the New Testament, that its spuriousness would be *prima facie* probable.

But, if we find no commandment in the New Testament which fits the case, we surely find none in the Old. We do, indeed, find there a commandment requiring the observance of a weekly Sabbath; but it is addressed, not to the Christian church, but to the Jewish church, and is obeyed more or less perfectly by the Jewish people to this day. The apostle Paul distinctly, and in more places than one, rejects the suggestion that that law is obligatory on him;

and while he might be willing to keep the weekly Sabbath, if it would be of any comfort to his brethren to have him do so, yet when anybody should undertake to make him keep it, or to insist that he was bound to keep it, he would give place to such an one by subjection, — no, not for an hour. All the energy of his manly Christian soul resented such a binding of his liberty; and he shook off the entanglement of that yoke. I do not see how any fair interpretation of passages in Paul's epistles like those which I read this morning (such as Col. ii. 16—iii. 11; Rom. xiv. 5, 6; and almost the whole of the Epistle to the Galatians), can avoid the conclusion that he, at least, regarded the commandment of the Sabbath as at an end.[1]

In that conclusion the whole Christian church has in practice, and for the most part in theory, acquiesced. In practice, I say: for, if the fourth commandment is obligatory, it is the seventh day which it enjoins; and the Christian church, with insignificant exceptions, has never observed the seventh day. And

[1] See especially Alford's long note on Col. ii. 16, 17.

in theory: for although some theologians before the Reformation regarded the law of the Sabbath as still in force,[1] only contriving in some illogical and unauthorized way to twist it from the seventh day to the first; and, although other theologians in the reformed church (not all of them, by any means, but some of them) have taken the same ground, — yet, on the whole, the verdict of the church has been most clearly in agreement with the verdict of the apostle Paul.

I confess, then, with the utmost frankness and honesty, that I can find no commandment, either in the New Testament or in the Old, obliging me to keep a weekly Sabbath. Not in the New: for there I am distinctly told to "let no man judge me" in respect of a holy day, . . . or of the Sabbaths; not only am I not obliged to keep them, but I am to resist those who would so oblige me. And not in the Old; for there I find a commandment addressed to Jews and not to Christians, and

[1] There is some doubtful trace of this opinion, as early as the third century, in Tertullian; but it was not till the sixth century that it became distinctly and formally declared. See Hessey's Third Lecture, especially pp. 77–96.

requiring, if it requires any thing, the observance of the seventh day and not the first.

It cannot be said in reply to this, that the law of the Sabbath, being a part of what is known as the Ten Commandments, distinguished by a peculiar dignity from the rest of the law, and graven expressly upon stone tables, remains permanent and binding upon all men, though the ceremonial law is passed away. To say this would be to beg the question; to say this would be expressly to gainsay the words of the apostle Paul already quoted. If the law of the Sabbath, as being a part of the Ten Commandments, had been permanently binding, Paul would hardly have taken pains to make obedience to it optional, as he distinctly does. Besides, where do we find any exception of these Ten Commandments from the acknowledged fulfilment or supersedure of the law by Christianity? It is the law as a whole that is superseded. Are we, then, to be told that this, by far the most important part of it, is still in force?

But some man will say that I am proving too much; that on this principle, and if the Ten Commandments are superseded, then I leave men free to steal, to kill, to commit adultery, to covet, and so on. To which the obvious answer is, that men are not left free to do these things; but it is because they are in conflict with the Spirit, not because they are in conflict with the commandment. The law was superseded by the Spirit. But even of the Spirit of life in Christ Jesus there is also a law, the law of liberty, the law of love. And there are some things on the stone tables, and some things in the parchment-books of Moses, which men everywhere and always are bound to observe. But why are they bound to observe them? Because they are graven on stone or written on parchment? No. But they were graven on stone or written on parchment because men are bound by the Spirit to observe them. I must not steal. Why must I not steal? Because it is so written in the Jewish law? No. But it is so written in the Jewish law, and in every other law, because I must not steal. It is wrong to kill. Why is it wrong to kill? Because the sixth commandment forbids killing? No. But the sixth commandment forbids killing because it is wrong to kill. My argument is not dangerous. It does not prove too much. And when I say that Christianity superseded the Jewish law, I mean, just as Paul meant, that it superseded the whole of the Jewish law. I may use portions of that law as a valuable and more or less perfect summary of universal moral duty. But I may not argue that this or that is universal moral duty, merely because I find it in that law. I say that it is safe to forbid stealing by an appeal to the Spirit of Christ. It is safe to forbid covetousness by an appeal to that love which is the living power of his kingdom. It is safe to ground all duty here, to rest all obligation here. If I can make an argument for a weekly Sabbath on this ground, then I can defend it. If I cannot, then my right to insist upon it must be abandoned. If I can show that the Spirit of Christ prompts any such observance; if I can show that love, which is the fulfilling of the law, — love to our God and Father, love to our Lord Jesus Christ, love to our brethren for whom he died, love to our own souls which he has purchased with his precious blood, — if, I say, I can show that love, which is the one great law, the only law of Christ, constrains us to this usage, or even that it finds a natural and helpful expression in this usage, — then I will urge it with all Christian zeal and by all fit methods. But, unless I can show this, I cannot urge it upon any man, any more than I could urge the feast of tabernacles or the rite of circumcision.[1]

I know that it will seem to some that I am taking much unnecessary trouble on myself, and that I am going by a circuitous and difficult course to my result, when there is the easy and short cut of the fourth commandment at my service. But I have lived long enough already to see the mischief of supporting a good cause by bad reasons, of defending truth by false argument, of risking battles in the maintenance of right by the use of wrong methods and by making a stand upon untenable positions. Of this error I desire not knowingly to be guilty. I desire, not merely to inculcate Christian truth, but to do it, so far as may be, with reasonable justification and explanation of it. And I know that it is never wise, that it is never right, to win a temporary victory for truth by winking out of sight an error.

[1] See note at the end of this sermon.

Therefore, in this and subsequent discourses, I rest my defence of our observance of the first day of the week, not on the fourth commandment, but on the law of love, on the Spirit of Christ. And after this long digression I come back to point out what significance the text has in this discussion, and what bearing on the important argument which I have taken in hand.

It is, as I said at the outset, one of the very few passages in the New Testament which indicate that the first day of the week was marked by the first disciples with any special observance. There is, as I say, no commandment requiring its observance; but is there, then, any evidence that the observance of it was a matter of general Christian usage? This text helps to answer the last question, and bears somewhat important testimony to the fact of such usage. The argument from it, in a word, is this: —

The apostle Paul and his travelling companions, going from Philippi to Ephesus, and so back from their missionary labors into Syria, came, after a voyage of five days from his last port, to Troas, where a little church of Christian disciples had been gathered. Here, says the story, told by one of the party, "we abode seven days," — the seven days closing with the first day of the week, — as if they had been waiting for the first day of the week to come for some special reason. What was the reason? "Upon the first day of the week, when we came together to·break bread" (the language seems to indicate an habitual act, — as if it were a thing of course that they should meet for worship and fellowship on that day), "Paul preached unto them, ready to depart" (or being about to depart) "on the morrow," — apparently having prolonged his stay especially for the sake of spending Sunday with the church, as if he knew that then would be the best of all opportunities for meeting them. Full of zeal and of enjoyment of their companionship, he continued his discourse till midnight, and even prolonged the communion season till daybreak. And so he departed, — commencing his journey before the Sunday had expired; for the day, of course, was counted from sunset to sunset. Two facts, then, seem taught by this incident. First, that the day was regarded as a day of religious privilege, even in apostolic days, and was sanctioned by apostolic example as an opportunity of religious assembly for worship and fellowship; and, secondly, that it was not regarded with any such strictness of obligation as that the apostle was hindered from commencing his journey upon it. Both of these facts are important.

But why was it regarded as a day of especial religious privilege? The answer is obvious. Already the division of time into weeks of seven days existed; and the fitness and convenience of this division were so great that it was never to be abandoned, but rather to become universal. Indeed, although the week of seven days comes to us and to the world from the Hebrew practice, it may even be said to be a natural division of time, founded upon the phases of the moon. At any rate, it is a division of time which has proved its fitness and convenience by the test of use; and all efforts which have been made to improve upon it — to make a week of ten days, for example, as in France during the time of her revolution — have signally failed. I say, then, that the week of seven days existed in the Jewish world, out of which the first Christians were gathered. Any great and memorable event, any event of singular and permanent gladness or of deep and abiding sorrow, occurring on the first day of any week, then, or on the fifth day of any week, would be remembered, as a matter of course, and by natural and inevitable association, when the first day or the fifth day of the next week would come around. And, if the event thus connected with that day was one of importance enough, it would be still remembered when the next week came, and when the next came, and the next. And if, perhaps, this great event connected with it was one of which the grandeur and significance grew no less but rather greater as the weeks and months and years rolled by; if it should prove to be an event so sublime, so transcendent, so full of gladness and promise and hope, that time could take away nothing from its meaning and glory, but could only add to it; if, also, it were an event which pointed forward all the time, as well as backward, requiring to be cherished, not as a memory only, but also, and even more constantly, as a prophecy, — then, as the day came around, each weekly observance of it would make the next more sure and more sacred, till the usage should become so venerable, so holy, so precious, that to touch it with the interference of rude hands would be a sacrilege intolerable. And when the day had won such sanctity as this, and reached such singular pre-eminence; when it had come to be so valued and beloved, by reason of its clustering associations, by all Christian souls; when with unanimous consent the church of Christ, which, as we have seen, is constantly inspired and guided by his living Spirit, had made the day a festival, — I think it would be as much ordained of God as if the ordinance had been written on the overarching skies, or graven on the everlasting hills. Is not the voice of the Christian people, in some true and proper sense, the voice of God?

Thus I indicate the line of argument to be employed. And now, very briefly, let us follow it out. We all know what was the one great event by which the first day of the week was made illustrious forever. It was the resurrection of the Lord Jesus Christ, the most sublime event in human history, the event which was the very keystone of that divine arch of promise by which the ruined world is spanned. On the first day of the week, he rose again from the dead. Do you suppose that group of sorrowing disciples who had spent the Jewish Sabbath in such depths of wondering despair, whose festival of rest had been turned, that week, into such weary gloom, whose last hope of the rest which Moses had spoken of, which Joshua had prefigured, which David had sung of, had flickered and gone out upon that gloomy seventh day, — do you think, I say, that they could ever possibly forget upon what day it was that there burst in upon their darkened souls the sudden and bewildering truth which turned their darkness into day, which kindled to new brightness the extinguished flame of hope, — which re-awakened all the expectation of a promised rest, — which opened up the very heavens to them in an infinite vista of glory? Could they ever forget what day it was that turned their sorrow into a joy that no man could thenceforth take from them; that made the most timid and distrustful of them resolutely bold, so that they went everywhere preaching "Jesus and the resurrection;" that furnished them thenceforward with their rallying cry, their most blessed gospel, their most resistless argument? Could they forget what day this was? Surely they could not forget it. They did not forget it. From the very first, there are indications that they marked it with peculiar emphasis. All the evangelists take pains to mention it as the day of resurrection. In John's Gospel it is recorded that the Lord appeared to his disciples at their assembly on the first recurrence of the resurrection day,— that is, on the eighth day after the day on which he rose, — marking it thus by peculiar honor. So we find, in this text, the assemblage on the first day of the week spoken of as if it were already a Christian usage. So elsewhere we find the apostle Paul advising that the first day of the week be used for charitable purposes. So we find the apostle John speaking of "the Lord's Day" as a recognized day, on which he was "in the Spirit."[1] Such hints as these we find in

---

[1] See Alford's interesting note on Rev. i. 10.

the New Testament, that, from the very first, it was impossible for the first day of the week to come without bringing to Christian men memories of sacred gladness, and welcome, and beautiful prophecies of hope. It pointed backward to the resurrection of the Lord, — a fact which only seemed to grow more glorious as, in the process of the weeks and years, it grew more distant. It pointed forward to their own resurrection, — a fact which grew more welcome and more real as, in the process of the weeks and years, it came more near.

Such hints as these, I say, we find in the New Testament, — such hints as these, and only these. I believe I have enumerated all of them. The verse which I have taken for a text is one of the strongest of them all, perhaps the very strongest.

But now, if any man will say that these few scattered hints, if they are all that the New Testament affords, furnish a very flimsy basis on which to rest the obligation to observe the first day of the week as a distinctly holy day, I quite agree with him. They do furnish a most insufficient ground on which to rest that obligation. I rest no such obligation on them. I hesitate to rest such obligation anywhere. I do not dare to use that word "obligation," lest I expose myself to the censure of the apostle Paul. If I go about obliging people to observe the first day, or the seventh day, or any other day, I seem to hear the stern voice of that great apostle saying over again to me what he said once to the churches of Galatia: "How turn ye again to the weak and beggarly elements whereunto ye desire again to be in bondage? Ye observe days and months and times and years. I am afraid of you, lest I have bestowed upon you labor in vain." I do not ground upon these texts, I cannot ground upon these texts, an obligation. I cannot find in them, or in any others, a commandment. But I do find in them a warrant for the privilege, a vindication of the right, to dignify the Lord's Day, and to hallow it. If I can make men see the worth of this privilege, if I can make men feel the value of this right, then I can even urge it on them as a duty. For, in Christ's kingdom, privilege is duty, and duty privilege. To his disciples, right involves responsibility.

The right of suffrage, for example, involves, as I have more than once insisted from this pulpit, the duty of suffrage. So the privilege of rest becomes to weary men the duty of rest. So the right to celebrate the weekly festival of the Lord's resurrection, and the weekly prophecy and promise of our own, devolves on tired and burdened men, immersed in care, and constantly surrounded by temptation and distracting evils, the responsibility of celebrating it with worship and repose. If the opportunity is given, — a day of religious opportunity, — the opportunity must be redeemed,[1] "because the days are evil."

Coming at it thus from the side of privilege, not as Jews, who still are bounden by the law, but rather as Christians to whom Christ has given the liberty of sons, the argument for the Lord's Day begins to take on shape and definiteness. That this is the true way to come at it, I have no doubt. That this is the way in which the Christian church came at it, is a matter of historic fact, and is even capable of historic proof.

[1] Eph. v. 16; where "redeeming the time" is, literally, "rescuing the opportunity."

For some years after the resurrection of our Lord, the Christian disciples were largely Jews, who had been trained under the law of Moses, and who had come to love the institutions, rites, and ordinances of the Hebrew church. To such, the immediate and complete abandonment of their Jewish customs was not easy nor desirable. If there were any who could not see their way clear to give up the rite of circumcision, they might keep the rite of circumcision for themselves and for their children; only they must not impose it upon others who could see no reason for it. Just as nowadays we say to any who cannot see their way clear to any form of baptism except immersion, Very well, you may employ that form if you desire, for yourselves; only you must not try to make us use it, if our conscience leaves us free to try some other mode. So with regard to the Jewish Sabbath. There were many who could not give it up. It was a privilege which they could not bear to surrender. It was a custom which they had so long employed, from childhood, always, everywhere, that they could not drop it. Very well, then, said the apostle, keep it. "He that regardeth the day regardeth it unto the Lord." But do not let him say to his brother Christian, who was perhaps brought up as a heathen, and who has no prejudice nor association nor preference connected with the weekly Sabbath, or who is a more instructed Jew, and recognizes that the Jewish Sabbath is no longer binding, — let him not say to such an one, "You must keep this seventh day with me." "Why dost thou judge thy brother?" cries the apostle: "He that regardeth not the day, to the Lord he doth not regard it."

So things went on for a while. The Jewish Christians, many of them, keeping the weekly Sabbath, the Gentile Christians keeping it not. Meantime, every week the first day came right after the seventh; and the associations of the first day grew, each week, more glad, more glorious, more holy. More and more it was felt to be a privilege to commemorate upon that day the sublime fact of the Lord's resurrection. More and more it came to be the custom, both of Jewish Christians and of Gentile Christians, to meet for worship and for fellowship upon that first day of the week. And thus it befell that presently the Jewish Christians found that they were really observing in each week two holy days instead of one. It was inevitable that presently the sanctity of one of them must wane. Many of the early Christians were slaves; almost all were poor men, working men. Two days out of a week could not be spared. It was an unnatural proportion. It wrought inconveniences of various sorts. In this busy world, not more than one-seventh of the time can be withdrawn for festivals, without disordering society. Easily enough, then, nay, inevitably, when the Jewish Christians were brought to the point, and forced to choose which of these two successive days they would surrender, they gave up the Jewish day. They found that already the festival of the Lord's resurrection had so strong a hold upon them, that they could not bear to give that up. Besides, by this time the Jewish Christians, who at first were the most numerous, had begun to be outnumbered, and the Gentile Christians, with their broader, **truer** views, had gained deserved ascendency.

I could cite quotations, if there were time, and if it were needful, from the very earliest Christian writers after the apostolic age, to verify this historical assertion. Among these are Ignatius and Justin Martyr,[1] who lived so close to apostolic times that they might even have known the last of the apostles personally. A passage attributed to Ignatius (which, however, is probably spurious) enjoins the keeping, both of Saturday and Sunday, but gives a marked preference to Sunday, as "the Lord's Day, as a festival, the queen and chief of all the days." But there is another version (confessedly authentic) of the same passage; and in this the writer dissuades from the observance of the Sabbath, and urges a life "according to the Lord's;"[2] the inference being, of course, that the practice of the church at that day was not settled and uniform. Some Christians kept the Sabbath; some observed the Lord's Day, and Ignatius was among the latter. And Justin says, that "Sunday is the day on which we all

---

[1] Ignatius died A.D. 107; Justin died A.D. 164.

[2] That is, "according to the Lord's life," as some interpret; or, as others interpret, "according to the Lord's Day."

hold our common assembly," the chief reason for it being that on that day "Jesus Christ our Saviour rose from the dead." I cite these two writers simply as representing the spirit of the Christian church upon this point during the first centuries of its history. I need not multiply citations.

There is not time to-day to prosecute the argument; and, if to any one it seems as yet incomplete, I pray him to remember that it does not claim to be complete, and ask him to reserve his judgment till it shall be finished. Two things only at this point I beg him to consider.

First, If it seems to him, as possibly it may seem to some, that the event which this first day of the week commemorates is scarcely so sublime or so important as to justify it in superseding the observance of the seventh day, let him look to it whether there is not something wrong in his theology. It did not seem so to the apostles, nor to the first disciples whom they gathered. One difference between the apostolic age and ours is just here evident. To them the resurrection was of all the facts in

Christian history the most illustrious. To some of us it is of no more than second-rate importance. Is there not something wrong here? Paul thought of Christ as of him "who died, yea, rather who is risen again." I have sometimes feared that we were suffering from some disproportion in the order of our doctrines concerning the Lord Jesus Christ, and that the doctrinal significance which we attach to the sacrificial death of Jesus had been somehow allowed to overshadow and obscure the glorious meaning of his resurrection. Is it not possible to linger so long by the cross and by the sepulchre as partly to deprive one's self of the glorious hopes and comforting assurances that attach themselves to the rising again from the dead? May not our Christian faith have been too much in a dead Christ, or rather, not enough in a living Christ? I have seen men stand at the sepulchre weeping, to whom I have longed to say, "He is not here: he is risen." These are grave considerations. But if it seems to us that the resurrection of the Lord is not of sufficient importance to justify the surrender of the seventh-day festival and the introduction of the first day in its place, let us find out whether our theology is not in need of some adjustment. This is the first point.

Secondly, If there is any man to whom this first day of the week comes, not as a day of Christian privilege, but as a day of burdensome obligation, or as a day without significance, let him ask whether something more than his theology is not at fault, whether his religion is not a failure. If, when the day which celebrates the resurrection of the Lord returns, it brings no meaning to you or to me; if, as it points backward to the sacred memories that cluster around the resurrection of the Lord, it stirs no thrill of gratitude in you and me; if we do not spring responsive to its summons to give thanks to him "who died, yea rather, who is risen again,"— then we may be sure that there is something wrong in us. Is it possible that Christ's resurrection is nothing to us? But surely it ought to be something to us. It is the earnest of our own immortality, the promise of our own resurrection. And the same day which points backward to the one points forward to the other. But perhaps the thought of your own resurrection, the assurance of your own immortality, has no attractiveness to you. Perhaps you give no heed to it, take no thought of it. Perhaps, even, it is an unwelcome thought to you, filling you, when it comes unsummoned, with gloomy doubts, harassing you with awful terrors. If this is so, men and brethren, if this is so with any of us, be sure that there is something deeper than mere theological error in us; that it is not merely intellectual ignorance and disorder that ails us; that it is a disordered and corrupt heart. I charge you, therefore, brethren, to beware of such an evil heart of unbelief toward the Lord Jesus Christ, lest, a promise being left us of entering into his rest, of sharing his immortality, and knowing the power of his resurrection, any of us shall seem to come short of it.[1]

[1] The custom of appealing to the Decalogue to sanction the observance of the Lord's Day seems to have grown up within the Roman church, in an age not remarkable for enlightenment and intellectual vigor. The growth of this practice has been sketched with some detail by recent English writers, especially by Dr. Hessey (in his third lecture), and by Dr. Reichel (quoted by Cox, vol. ii. pp. 380-384). It is not too much to say that the view of the fourth commandment which is taken in this and the following sermons, has the greatest and most authoritative names in church history upon its side.

To those of us who have been used to insist that the Decalogue is still obligatory, and the Mosaic Sabbath still in force, the writings, even of Luther and of Calvin, must seem loose and perilous; while the whole catalogue of German scholars, almost without exception, the devout and evangelical as well as the rationalistic, give one unbroken testimony in the same direction. Not less emphatic is the opinion of the most accomplished English exegetes, like Alford; and of men like Whately, and Thomas Arnold, and Frederick Robertson, and a host of others. Very significant, also, is the fact that devout scholars on the continent of Europe, recognizing the superior excellence of the Lord's Day as observed in America, are urging the introduction of our practice, while they continue to condemn our theory.

V.

THE LORD'S DAY HONORABLE.

"For if that which is done away was glorious, much more that which remaineth is glorious." — 2 Cor. iii. 11.

IN the sermon which I preached a week ago, we passed from the discussion of the Jewish Sabbath to the examination of the Christian festival of the Lord's Day. I trust that it was made sufficiently evident, in the course of that sermon, that these two days are not the same, but different in many respects. Before we rest from this discussion, I desire to acknowledge, that in certain other respects there is important similarity between them also; but the points of similarity and comparison will be better appreciated if the points of difference and contrast shall be first and fully recognized.

It will be remembered that I frankly disclaimed any wish to rest the observance of our Christian festival upon the fourth commandment, and even that I was at some pains to show why that commandment could not properly be quoted as applying to this observance: because it was a Jewish statute, not a Christian one; because, however excellent and admirable, however august in its enactment and divine in its authority, it still was local, transient, partial, and has been superseded by the universal, permanent, and perfect spirit of our Lord Jesus Christ. I know that it will seem to some a shorter and easier way to call this Lord's Day the Sabbath day, and to invoke the sanction of the statute written on stone tables to sustain the observance of it. I know that this may even seem a stronger ground on which to rest the observance, because it has the thunders of the fiery mountain back of it, and because (I say it sorrowfully) the stone of Sinai sometimes seems to our dull senses stronger and more divine than the unseen spirit of the New Testament.

Brethren, I do not wish to take away one ray of glory from this law of Moses; and I could not if I would. Sublime indeed with an august and awful glory is that mountain of the law, burning with fire and hidden in the blackness and darkness and tempest, and echoing with "the sound of the trumpet and the voice of words;" terrible with a divine glory, that theophany at which Moses said, "I exceedingly fear and quake." Glorious indeed was the graven law on the stone tables given to be the constitution of the Jewish state. What earthly state had ever yet a constitution comparable for a single moment with it in glory? Glorious, too, with the high glory of an inspired wisdom were the laws and statutes written in conformity with this grand constitution; glorious the institutions and the ordinances which grew up around and under it, — the ritual, the festivals, the holy places, and the holy seasons of the Jewish people. Glorious with a peculiar glory were the Jewish Sabbaths, weekly Sabbaths, monthly Sabbaths, Sabbaths of years, culminating in the great semi-centennial Sabbath jubilee. All this was very glorious. I would not speak one word that should detract from it, that should, even in appearance, lessen it. I rather magnify and emphasize it; knowing all the time, that from it, as from solid vantage ground, we shall rise so much the higher when we come to estimate the glory of the Christian church, the beauty of the city of the living God, the length and breadth and height of the New Jerusalem. "For if that which was done away is glorious, much more that which remaineth is glorious."

For it is done away, — this glorious structure of the Jewish state, this sacred temple of the Jewish church. It is done away, — constitution graven on stone tables, statutes written upon venerable rolls, the temple, with its august ritual, the festivals, with all the glory of their memory and prophecy, the humane civil ordinances as to meat and drink and cleanliness, the holy days, the new moons, and the Sabbaths. The language of the great apostle, in the text and elsewhere, is most unequivocal upon this point. This was the very point on which the church at Corinth, to which he was writing, was plagued and imperilled at that very time. There had come to it certain teachers representing zealously the Jewish party in the Christian church, — that party of which I spoke a week ago as insisting upon the observance of Jewish rites and ceremonies (such as the rite of circumcision), and of Jewish festivals, such as the weekly Sabbath. Not content with these observances for themselves, to whom, as Jews by birth and education, they were natural and valuable, they insisted that the Gentile churches, such as this one at Corinth, should be forced to keep them also; which, when Paul denied, they went so far as even to dispute his apostolical authority, and challenged his doctrine as broad and dangerous, and his life as lax and disorderly. Against such charges and insinuations, the apostle, in his letter, vehemently defends himself; and so, incidentally, has need to refer again and again to the relation between the gospel and the law, between the new covenant and the old, between the ministration of Christ and the ministration of Moses. Both are glorious, he says; but the glory of the new is infinitely the greater. He does not honor Moses less, but he adores Christ more. He does not undervalue or contemn the Jewish law; but, when he puts it by the side of the glorious gospel of the Lord, it fades into invisibility by the comparison. Even the sacred constitution of the Jewish state and church is not excepted, "written and engraven in stones" (we know what portion of the law this was), even this was done away by being superseded. You do not need a candle at high noon. You cannot see it if you have it. It has "no glory in this regard, by reason of the glory that excelleth." So with the Jewish law: you pay no fit honor to it when you insist that it is still in force, — nay, that it is in force more really and extensively than ever. Exaggerated honor is dishonor. The true way to reverence it is the apostle's way. Admit the glory of it, — partial, temporary, local. And then lift your eyes to see the glory of the New Testament, the ministration of the Spirit.

Approaching the subject thus fearlessly, but without the least irreverence, I hope to show in the particular case which I have taken in hand, how our Lord's Day has greater glory than the Jewish Sabbath. Only let us first complete and fortify the argument for its observance. For since the law written and engraven in stones, with all its glory, is done away, we have no right to rest the argument on the commandment. And, since the living Spirit of the Lord prompts the observance, we have no need to rest the argument on the commandment, but appeal directly to the liberty of love. Does the love of Christ constrain us to it? Does the love of God, the love of man, the love of our own souls, impel us to the voluntary commemoration of this first day of the week? Or does this love find fit and useful expression in such a commemoration?

(1) The question is threefold. Does love to Christ constrain us? The answer is not hard to find. I showed, a week ago, how naturally, how inevitably, from the very first, the earliest disciples marked the day of the Lord's resurrection, as week by week it came around. They could not help it. It would have been hard not to mark it. So profoundly had the risen Lord become endeared to them, so sublimely had he proved his power and Godhead to them, so mysteriously near and present to them had he come to be, by rising from the dead, that, by an irresistible impulse, they met to speak of that great victory, and to worship the divine Victor on the first day of the week,

on which day he arose. At first the resurrection reminded them of the day. But presently the day began to remind them of the resurrection; and they doubtless found a comfort in their trials, and an encouragement in their faith, as week by week this eloquent commemoration was repeated. The lapse of time, the things of sense, must by and by have dimmed the memory and dulled the souls, even of men whose eyes had seen the Lord. For they were in the flesh and in the world, with fleshly hinderances to faith, with worldly liabilities to forgetfulness. For them, even though "with mortal eyes" they had "beheld the Lord," it was sometimes hard to remember, it was often easy to forget. So, with a natural instinct, they stretched out their hands of faith to grasp supports of any kind that would sustain and comfort. Such a support was the Lord's Day, speaking perpetually of his death, of his resurrection, of his coming again to raise them also; speaking perpetually, with the pathetic eloquence of memory, with the inspiring eloquence of prophecy, of him "that liveth and was dead, and, behold, he is alive forevermore!"

So, to each successive generation of disciples did this weekly festival prove its own value and establish its own sanctity. It made them think of Christ, — of Christ, whom thus to think of is to love the more. For the working of this principle is the same in either way that we may take it. If we love him we must think of him. If we think of him we must love him. If we love him deeply it will help us to connect the thought of him with every thing, with every place, with every time. If we connect the thought of him with every thing, with every place, with every time, we shall love him the more deeply. The truth of this is obvious; and the principle is one so natural, so irresistible, that we are acting upon it more or less unconsciously all the time. We even call it a law, the law of association; only it is applied here in the most sacred and important of all applications. So that the law of association may properly be called a law of the Lord's Day. And no love that is real and intelligent will consent to disobey it.

But at first, before the life and habits of the Christian church had come to be well defined and adjusted, there was some risk of carrying this law of association to an extreme and inconvenient application. At first the Christian disciples tried to make of every day a Lord's Day; as indeed it ought to be, in some fit and proper sense: they would make of the week, and of the year, a commemoration of the earthly life of the Lord Jesus. It has been well said by Robertson of Brighton,[1] "they set, as it were, the clock of time to the epochs of his history." Friday, for instance, brought to mind the day of his death. Saturday was the day of his entombment. Sunday was the day of his resurrection; and so on, through the week and through the year. All this was well. It sprung from a devout thought and purpose. It is right for faith to catch at every thing by which to stay itself; for memory to prop itself, for hope to lift itself, by all such means. Only there must presently come in other considerations, other influences, other necessities, to modify this practice.

So, as a matter of fact, the observance of Friday grew more and more unimportant, grew

[1] Sermons, vol. ii. p. 203.

less and less strict and universal, though it lingers to this day among the most numerous sections of the Christian church; the observance of Saturday became obsolescent, and at last obsolete; but the observance of Sunday has grown more and more important, more and more universal, more and more glorious as the church has endured. What is the reason of this fact?

The reason of it is partly this, — that the importance of the resurrection as the culminating fact in the earthly history of the Lord Jesus, as the last link in the chain of evidence which proved his Godhead, as the keystone of the arch of gospel promise, fitly gave the resurrection day pre-eminence above the others. And it presently began to be discovered that a formal, general observance of them all as fasts or festivals would be impossible. To observe all days alike would answer very well, if all days alike would give the opportunity for rest from worldly occupation, and for fellowship and worship. But this could not be. Some days must be employed in busy work from dawn till dusk, with toiling hand and anxious heart. It was not every day that could be rescued for the special and peculiar uses of religion and of charity. It must be one of several days. The structure of the week as a natural and inherited division of time, pointed to one in seven as the true proportion between rest and labor. Probably this, also, is the proportion indicated by God in the nature and constitution of man. One day in seven has been tried for centuries, and has worked well. There are on record one or two experiments of peoples who have tried some other proportion. One day in ten was tried in France, but unsuccessfully. It is difficult for science, which in such a case must depend upon experiment for its facts, to speak with positive assertion on this point. But men without religious prejudices to impel them one way or another, have pronounced that the proportion between holidays and work-days, between rest and labor, is best met by the venerable Jewish custom of one in seven. Less than that tends to drudgery and dulness and degradation, and so is inhuman. More than that tends to idleness and thriftlessness, and so is wasteful. Of the first effect, examples are abundant in all heathen lands, where the incessant round of toil, unbroken by a seventh day of rest and religious observance, grinds down to uniform debasement the faces of the poor. Of the second result, examples may be found, sufficiently significant, in certain Christian lands where religious festivals have come to be so numerous and frequent, that, by reason of them, the orderly, industrious, and thrifty pursuit of business becomes well nigh impossible. Any one who has ever been in Rome, for instance, will remember how fatal to habits of industry and to successful business are the innumerable holidays which interrupt the week, and break into irregularity the order of the year. There are so many sacred days, so many rest-days, that the Lord's Day, properly so called, loses its value and sanctity, and the people waste their time in idleness and worse. Practically, then, we may even say that it seems to be partly proved by experiment that one day in seven taken from the care of business and from the drudgery of toil is good for men; that less than this is not enough, and leaves them dull and tired; and that more than this is too much, and makes them lazy and inert.

But this proportion, justified apparently by practical experiment, was first suggested to us by the Jewish lawgiver. We owe it to the Hebrew church. And just in proportion as science proves it natural and necessary, just in that proportion do we get the fuller proof of the high inspiration by which Moses was directed. In choosing this proportion he was not led by accident, he was led by God. He found it hinted in the very order of God's own creation : six days of wise creative labor, and a seventh day of holy rest. God showed him this divine proportion, and he copied it ; and by copying it has made the world, which is adopting it, his debtor.

This fact, then, helps to explain why it was that Friday and Saturday and the other days of the week presently lost their constant association with particular incidents in the life of the Lord Jesus, while Sunday, the first day of the week, retained it. The observance of the other days with any formal celebration was impossible for men who had to labor for their daily bread. It deranged the true proportion between days of rest and days of work. If two days in seven had been possible, they would very likely have observed Friday as a general fast-day, and Sunday as a general feast-day. But since they were shut up by circumstances, and by nature even, to one day in seven, of course they chose to keep the first, the festival of the Lord's resurrection. Their love to him constrained them to employ the day as a reminder of his risen life, his constant presence.

Not less, my friends, not less the love of Christ constraineth us. Do we remember him with so much diligence and constancy that we desire no aids to memory, no incentives to our diligence, no confirmation of our constancy? When a friend beloved is taken from our side by death, with what instinctive eagerness do we treasure every association that will help to keep his memory fresh and green. This was his birthday, we remember, — this was the day he died. Here is his portrait, here the house in which he lived, here the green grave in which his body sleeps. Our love and fealty to our friend suggest these reminiscences, constrain us to these eloquent and powerful associations. Deliberately to put them by and forbid ourselves the use of them, seems to argue a willingness to forget, a waning of our love, a shallowness in our regret.

Just so, because we love our Lord, we love the day that makes us think of him. Does any man reply with disavowal of his love to Christ, and say, "I do not profess to love the Lord, and therefore I do not love the day that makes me think of him." Strange as it seems, there are those who will make this disavowal and excuse. But to such men the necessity of such a day as this is all the greater. You ought to love the Lord who loved you unto death, who loves you still with a pathetic agony of yearning love ; you ought to love him, and you need to be reminded of him till you do. The value of the day to you is all the greater for the very reason which you urge against it. There is a risen Lord, a living Lord, a loving Lord, who died for you, who lives for you, who is coming to you in judgment. You need to think of him. You must love him, for his love is drawing you. Here is a day that naturally speaks of him. You ought to listen to it. It is fraught with clustering memories of him and of his love. You need to heed them. It is bright with thronging promises of him and of his power. You must not refuse them.

Perhaps I have dwelt long enough upon this first division of my question. Does that love which is the spirit of the gospel prompt us to the observance of the first day of the week? Does love to Christ constrain us to it? Yes, I say. Love to him would prompt us, if we could, to link every day to him by some particular and potent association. But, if this cannot be done, then love to him constrains us to link any day we can to him by such perpetual and potent law. Here is a day which we can so employ. The natural necessities of body and of mind permit, nay, even require, one day in seven for such use as this. And so the argument is perfect. "This is the day which the Lord hath made: we will rejoice and be glad in it."

(2) But the love which is the spirit of the gospel burns broad as well as high; reaches

not only to the heavens, reaches also unto all the earth; looks upward to the living Lord, looks outward to our fellow-men. Does love to man constrain us, then, to the observance of this festival of the Lord's Day?

It is not hard to answer. If our love to men constrains us to desire that they shall know and love the Lord who died for them, it must impel us to supply them with all useful means and opportunities to know and love him. This is a busy world. The cares of poverty are many and corroding. The deceitfulness of riches is a very evil thing. Labor and anxiety and sorrow, trial and temptation and fatigue, well nigh to death, — these occupy the time of men, absorb the thoughts of men, busy the hearts of men; and Christ is shut out from the souls he came to save and sanctify, because there is no room for him to enter, because there is no moment when he can be heard. On the plain ground of expediency, then, we might safely rest the observance of one day in seven as a day of Christian opportunity. Even if you did not need it for yourself, nor I for myself, it would be our duty, in the absence of all reason to the contrary, to supply this opportunity to those who needed it for themselves. Putting it upon the very lowest ground, even, as a day of physical rest and recreation, it would be the dictate of a wise and Christian expediency to provide for its observance. And Christian expediency, when it is clearly recognized, comes to be Christian obligation; just as, by the law of Christ, privilege is no way different from duty, nor duty different from privilege. I say, then, that the Lord's Day, as a day of Christian opportunity, is an expedient so wise, so useful, so successful, that the love to man which is inspired by Christ, which is the spirit of Christ, constrains us to the observance of it. Indeed, this seems to me so evident, that I need scarcely dwell upon it further.

(3) But the love which we owe to our own souls constrains us to the same result. We are to love our neighbors as ourselves. For us too, as for all men, Christ has died. And, since our souls are precious in his sight, they must be precious in our own. I say, then, that you need this day, and that I need it. If you and I were

wholly spiritual, then all time might be alike to us. But we are not wholly spiritual. We are not out of the body : we are in the flesh. We are tired, and we need to rest. We are thronged with earthly cares, and we need sometimes to lay them by. We are tempted to forgetfulness of Christ, and we need to be reminded of him. Taking the day upon the lowest ground, again, as an opportunity of physical and mental rest, we need it. Your physician will prescribe it for you as a necessary aid to bodily and mental health. But we need it even more, as an opportunity for worship and fellowship, for "the assembling of ourselves together" for mutual helpfulness, for the breaking of bread, for works of charity, for the joyful anticipation of our perfect rest. Each one of us is tired enough to value it. If we are not, we ought to be. It argues idleness and worthlessness on our part if we are not ready for this rest when it returns. Each one of us is tired enough, tempted enough, distracted enough, tied down to earth enough, to love the day which gives us opportunity for looking into heaven. When we cease to be tired and tempted and earthbound, it will be soon enough to raise the question of dispensing with this opportunity; when the days cease to be evil, it will be soon enough to neglect to redeem this time. Till then we need it. Till then it is our privilege. Till then, therefore, the Spirit of our Lord, the love which is the law and power of his kingdom, will constrain us to its observance. Till then it will help to make his presence real to us, his life, his death, his resurrection real.

Resting here the argument for the observance of the Lord's Day upon such various, and I presume to say such firm and solid, bases, I have left myself but little space to indicate in what respects the glory of this Christian festival is greater than the glory of the Jewish. Certain points of similarity between the two, as well as certain points of contrast, have incidentally appeared in the progress of the discussion. They are not the same. The one was on the seventh day of the week. The other is on the first day of the week. The one had for its occasion a conspicuous incident in the history of a nation. The other has for its occasion the central fact in the history of mankind. The one was a monumental day to mark the emancipation of a race of slaves. The other is a monumental day that marks the rescue of a world of sinners. The one rests on a stern commandment, graven on stone tables, given with terrific and almost intolerable majesty of visible sight and audible sound. The other rests upon the free spirit of a willing and loving discipleship, a spirit unwritten, invisible, the living, loving Spirit of the living Lord himself. The one is local. The other is fast coming to be universal.

So much by way of contrast. But there is comparison as well. Both days were festivals. The Jewish Sabbath, as I took pains to show in the third of these discourses, was not by any means a bondage. It was a privilege, a glad day, the poor man's day, the slave's day. So is our Christian festival a privilege, a glad day, a day for toil to cease, a day for recreation and rejoicing, a day for the poor in spirit, for the meek and lowly. Both have been subjected to the same abuse, — have been twisted into burdensome yokes, — have been made a toil instead of a repose. Both days are Sabbath days in some lower usage of the word, but neither is the real and perfect Sabbath. That is eternal in the heavens. Both days are days of memory. Both speak of slavery, — one of the slavery of Egypt, the other of the slavery of sin. Both speak of rescue from slavery, — one of the rescue wrought by God through Moses, the other of the rescue wrought by God in Christ. Both days preach lessons of humility: one spoke to Israel of their low estate, and bade them never to forget that they were slaves, helpless and hopeless, till God rescued them; the other speaks to all men of their lost condition, and bids them never to forget that they were dead in trespasses and sins, helpless and hopeless, till Christ died for them. Both days are days of prophecy and promise. Both are days of rest, and speak of higher and more perfect rest. Both days are gilded with the brightness of a coming glory, growing brighter as it comes the nearer. The one, "illusively" leading the expectations of the restless people on from Moses to Joshua, from Joshua to David, from David to the Son of David; the other, leading the expectations of the waiting world onward and upward through the rolling ages, and above the changing earth, to Him who all the while is coming again in the power of his own resurrection. The first day prophesied the second, and the second typifies the last. Both days are glorious with the glory which streams in from the invisible; but just as of two mountain peaks, the highest one will catch the grandest splendor of the sunlight and hold it longest: so of these, the Christian festival has glory so excelling, that, by comparison with it, the other is not glorified. Both days are temporary and transient, for "they reckon not by years and days" within the veil. One of them is done away already. The other yet remains. And if that which is done away was glorious, much more that which remaineth is glorious.

Chiefly in these three respects it has pre-eminent glory beyond that of the Jewish Sabbath. I need only point them out in closing, for I have dwelt upon them already by anticipation; and I leave every man to ponder them in his own thoughts.

This first. The Christian festival is a free day. Its service is a willing service. It rests upon no stony statute. It is the spontaneous, unforced act of loving discipleship. And its glory in this regard is so much greater than the glory of the Jewish day, as the liberty of love is greater than the bondage of the law; as the ministration of the Spirit is more glorious than the ministration of the letter.

And this day, secondly, is more glorious than the other by reason of its universality. That was local — for one nation. This is fast becoming universal. Already it is accepted as a welcome privilege by Christian nations many and populous. And whenever in his stately goings, the Lord Christ comes in the knowledge of his gospel to new nations and new lands, on distant continents or in the islands of the sea, he brings this privilege with him, — imposing it on none, permitting it to all. And so, by an increasing multitude which no man can number, it is coming to be valued and observed; and weary sons of toil look up from the long bondage of unremitted drudgery, and give thanks for the day which gives them liberty and rest; and souls long-laboring and heavy laden with the tiresome yoke of sin rejoice to celebrate the day which promises a rest remaining for the people of God. So that soon, as year by year the kingdom of our Lord advances, there shall be no land or nation, no kindred or people, where this day shall not commemorate the resurrection of the Lord, and prophesy the rest which, in the power of his resurrection, he is giving and shall give to men.

And this suggests the third respect in which the glory of this day is greater than the glory of the Jewish day, — its increased spirituality. The Jewish day, indeed, pointed to heaven and to God, but pointed indirectly and remotely, pointed through types and shadows and intervening clouds. It spoke of heaven; but it spoke of Moses first, of Joshua, of David, and through them of heaven. But this day points directly upward, through no media, but straight into the opening heaven, to Christ who died, yea rather, who is risen again, and who is coming in his risen power to give us rest with him, to give us rest in him. We know where our rest is. We know how our rest is. We look to him. And this day speaks to us directly, potently of him.

To-day, then, brethren, if ye will hear his

voice, harden not your hearts; and see that ye refuse not him that speaketh — that speaketh on his holy day and by it. For by as much as our heavenly Jerusalem is more glorious than the awful mount that burned with fire, by so much is the eloquence and pathos of this day more mighty than the teaching of the Jewish Sabbath. Let there not be, my brethren, let there not be in us, in any one of us, an evil heart of unbelief, lest, a promise being left us of entering into rest, of sharing in the glory of Christ's resurrection, any of us should seem to come short of it.

VI.

THE RIGHT OBSERVANCE OF THE LORD'S DAY.

"𝕷𝖊𝖙 𝖊𝖛𝖊𝖗𝖞 𝖒𝖆𝖓 𝖇𝖊 𝖋𝖚𝖑𝖑𝖞 𝖕𝖊𝖗𝖘𝖚𝖆𝖉𝖊𝖉 𝖎𝖓 𝖍𝖎𝖘 𝖔𝖜𝖓 𝖒𝖎𝖓𝖉."
Rom. xiv. 5.

IT may have seemed to some, as they have listened to the sermons in which, during the last few weeks, I have discussed the relation of the Jewish Sabbath to the Christian festival of the Lord's Day, and the relation of both of these rest-days to the eternal Sabbath of the living God, — it may have seemed to some, I say, that the tendency of the argument was rather to unsettle the minds of men, — and that, too, upon a most important and practical matter, — than to persuade them fully concerning their own personal duty. To such persons it seems a grievous evil that the minds of men should be unsettled on so grave a subject. No doubt it is. And no doubt the apostle Paul would so regard it; since we here find him, speaking on this very point, deprecating any such unsettlement of conviction, and urging, "Let every man be fully persuaded in his own mind." The word used is a very strong and emphatic one. The meaning is, that every man should carefully and clearly settle the question of duty in his own convictions. Let him be fully persuaded, and let him be fully persuaded in his own mind.

It is not difficult to see where the danger is if questions of this sort are left unsettled. The apostle himself indicates it a little farther on. Scruples of conscience can never be disregarded safely; and, therefore, scruples of conscience ought not to be unnecessarily multiplied. To think that a thing is wrong is to make it wrong to him who thinks so. "He that doubteth," says the apostle, with regard to the vexed question of meats offered to idols, "He that doubteth is damned if he eat." To eat is not wrong: to refrain from eating is not wrong. But to eat when one thinks he ought not to eat is wrong: to refrain from eating when one thinks he ought to eat is wrong.

The spirit with which the thing is done is what gives it its character. It is the conscience of the man that must be kept void of offence. If it be an ignorant or mistaken conscience, still it is conscience, and must not be wounded. If the light it gives is broken and imperfect light, it must still be followed. It is to be enlightened by all possible means, cleansed, strengthened, instructed, — certainly ; but meantime it is to be followed, what there is of it, and used as best it may be. To act in opposition to it, or in disregard of it, is to incur spiritual injury and damage of a very serious sort.

This is the position which the apostle takes, and it commands assent the moment it is stated. All men agree that a man must act according to the light he has ; and, if he does so, we hold him blameless. Walking in the twilight, I may see what seems to be a dangerous pit : if it so seems to me by this twilight, according to the best judgment I can form, of course I must keep clear of it. Returning by and by, at noonday, I discover that it is not a perilous pit at all, but a harmless shadow. Now I am not bound to keep clear of it, but pass directly over it. So conscience may bind me to do one thing to-day; but to-morrow, being better instructed, it may bind me to do the opposite thing. Or my conscience may bind me to one course, and your conscience, being differently instructed, may bind you to the opposite course. And so we may have, and often do have, the spectacle of two equally good men, equally conscientious men, doing two diverse and even directly antagonistic acts. In such a case the danger is (first), that they will judge one another by the light each one of his own conscience; whereas that is sufficient only for the judgment of one's self, and not for the judgment of one's neighbor: or else (secondly), that they will disregard each one his own conscience, and adopt each one his neighbor's. The danger is twofold. Let me state it again still more simply. I may impose my conscience on my neighbor, and say, "What is wrong for me is wrong for you," and therefore condemn him. Or I may adopt his conscience for myself, and say, "What is right for you is right for me," and therefore follow him, to the damage of my own soul. In either case I greatly err. For I forget that each man's conscience is his own, and no one's else. It binds no one but him. But him it does bind.

Hence the importance of settling questions of duty clearly, firmly, intelligently, — not by force, but by persuasion; and not for other people, not for everybody once for all, but each one for himself, every man in his own mind. Unless this be done, this double danger of judging our brother, on the one hand, and of being made to offend by our brother, on the other hand, is very present and very constant. When a man is fully persuaded in his own mind concerning his own duty he will be safe against both perils. He will respect the conscience of other men because he respects his own; and, if they differ with him, he will neither judge them nor be judged by them. But if he has no firm convictions of his own, he will suffer constant damage. He is querulous on the one hand, and timorous on the other. He does a thing, and presently chides himself for fear that it was wrong, and so begins to abstain from doing it. Or he abstains from a thing, and presently grumbles because he sees other people doing it with no sense of wrong, and so begins to do it himself. "I don't know that it is right," he says, and yet he does it; and so his conscience worries him, and ought to worry him. "I don't know that it is wrong," he says; and yet he does not do it, and so he is chafed and fretted with his bondage. Either way he has no liberty, no peace; and the only way for him to secure liberty and peace and safety is to follow the counsel of the apostle in this text, "Let every man be fully persuaded in his own mind." Let him be settled in his convictions.

But some things never can be settled till they are settled right. To settle a question of conscience by force, for instance, — by external pressure of command and authority, — is no way to settle it. Settle it that way, and, as soon as the pressure of outside force is taken off, it will present itself again. It is to be settled, not violently, but intelligently; not by an appeal to arbitrary statutes, but by an appeal to eternal principles; not by referring it to the letter which killeth, but to the spirit which giveth life. Let a man be persuaded in his own mind.

Let him see the reason of the thing. Let him see on what unchanging principles it rests. Let it be settled by intelligent persuasion, not by unreasoning compulsion. Then it will stand.

And "every man in his own mind." Let the settlement be a personal one. Let me remember that I am deciding for myself, and not for my neighbor; and that he is deciding for himself, and not for me. "Every one of us shall give account of himself to God," — of himself, not of his neighbor. Each before his Judge, in the court of his own conscience, stands or falls. It will be a great comfort to us if we bear this fact in mind. It will save us a great deal of worry and care. We need not decide questions of duty for other people. We cannot decide them for other people. Some people think that this is what a minister is for, to decide questions of casuistry for his congregation. I always refuse to do it. Every one in his own mind, and for himself, must settle them. Principles are the same, always, and to all; but how to apply principles each man must determine for himself. I can give advice, experience, sympathy, help; but, in the end, I cannot take off from any man's conscience its own personal responsibility. To fetter him in his own determinations is spiritual tyranny of the most intolerable sort. To inflict it is a cruel wrong. And good men have gone to the stake and the gallows rather than submit to it.

Having now drawn out the meaning of the text, I wish to apply it to the question which we have had under discussion. It almost applies itself sufficiently. Depend upon it, this Sabbath question never will be settled till it is settled right; never will cease to be a perplexing question till the argument for it is based, as I have tried to base it, on right principles; never will cease to be a painful question, causing censoriousness on one side and offence on the other, till it is recognized as being a matter, not for general and obligatory commandment, but for the individual conscience. And if the argument which I have been conducting has tended to unsettle anybody's mind, I justify myself by saying that it has been with the hope and purpose that thereby such a person's mind might be settled right again, and settled permanently, in Christian faith and Christian charity.

That most thoughtful and Christian preacher whom I have had occasion to quote already, once or twice, in the course of this discussion, Robertson of Brighton, has pointed out the fact [1] that hardened criminals have sometimes traced their career in crime to the breaking of the Sabbath day as its first step. But, as he observes with fine discernment, the inference which we sometimes draw from such a confession is unwarranted. We sometimes infer, that, because the criminal confesses that his breaking of the Sabbath was a sin to him, therefore it must be sin to every one and everywhere. Whereas, this does not follow. It only follows that the criminal wounded his own conscience. He did a thing which he thought was wrong. To him, therefore, it was wrong. Whether it is wrong to other people or not, is still an open question.

So, I dare say, many of us have, at one time or another, sinned in the same way. If

[1] Sermons, vol. ii. p. 210.

we regard the Jewish law of the Sabbath as still in force, then we are bound to obey it, and to obey the whole of it. If we are fully persuaded in our own minds that the fourth commandment is a statute for us, then disobedience to the fourth commandment is for us a grievous sin. And yet I doubt if there is one of us who keeps that fourth commandment: it designates the seventh day; have we never had scruples concerning the seventh day? Have we ever fully persuaded our own minds concerning the twist by which this law is made applicable to the first day? Have we not sometimes doubted whether we were not bound to fall in with the Seventh-day Baptist sect in their observance of Saturday? And doubting thus, but not regarding our doubts, have we not damaged our consciences?

Or, if no one pleads guilty on this point, let us look still farther. "In it thou shalt not do any work,"—this is the language of the command,—"in it thou shalt not do any work, thou, nor thy son, nor thy daughter, nor thy manservant, nor thy maidservant, nor thy cattle, nor thy stranger that is within thy gates." Do we obey this law? It is a strict law; it is a plain law; it is easy to understand it; it is hard to evade it. "Not any work." Do you do no work on Sunday? I do not ask whether you do less work than on week-days. I ask whether you do no work. Do you never write a letter? Do you never busy your brain with cares of business? Do you never work with hand or foot? Carry the question farther still. Does your man-servant or your maid-servant not do any work on Sunday except what is dictated by mercy or necessity? Do you never stretch those words "mercy and necessity" to cover somewhat multitudinous exceptions? Carry the question farther still. Do your cattle do no work on Sunday? Do you make no use of your horses except what necessity or mercy dictates? Brethren, I do not believe that any one of us, tried by the standard of this Jewish law, could plead not guilty. We allow ourselves in things which we believe that it condemns.

What then? Do I say that no man must use his horse on Sunday; that no man must suffer food to be cooked in his house on Sunday; that no man may walk on Sunday except as mercy or necessity requires; that no man may put forth his hand or employ his brain in work, for recreation, for example, or for expediency of any sort, — do I say this? No: because I do not hold the fourth commandment as obligatory. If I did, I should say this. If you do, you are bound to do this. And if you recognize your obligation to do this, and do it not, you wound your conscience and do damage to your soul. And here is the point. Our theory concerning the Lord's Day is in conflict with our practice. Our theory concerning it is, that the law of the Jewish Sabbath applies to it. Our practice is to use it with more or less of Christian liberty. What shall we do, then? Our Christian instincts urge us to liberty. Our Jewish traditions entangle us with a yoke of bondage. The spirit seems to justify our freedom. The letter seems to condemn it. Our practice does not seem to us wrong, when we look into the Gospels and the epistles. But it does not seem to us right, when we look into the books of Exodus and Deuteronomy. We condemn ourselves in that which we allow. We eat, but doubt. And the wear and tear of conscience in the process is serious and perilous. What shall we do, then? Manifestly, this is the first thing to be done: "Let every man be fully persuaded in his own mind." Take the question up fearlessly and honestly. Find out which is right, our theory or our practice. Settle the point.

But how settle it? Suppose we cannot settle it. Suppose, when all the light possible has been gained by study, people's minds will disagree. Suppose, when all is done, the practice of the Christian world is still not uniform. Suppose it to be true of us, as it was of the church at Rome in Paul's day, that "one man esteemeth one day above another; another esteemeth every day alike." What then?

The case is not a hypothetical one with us. It is a very real, a very important, a very embarrassing one. We of New England, our fathers who are buried there, and we who turn with loving hearts and reverent memory thither, as to the source and fount of what is best and truest in the nation, — our fathers and ourselves (with some eminent exceptions) have been accustomed to regard the Lord's Day as commanded by the Jewish law, and to quote that law as the authority for its observance. On the other hand, good men in Germany and elsewhere, devout and learned men, have been accustomed to regard the Jewish law as superseded, and to observe the Lord's Day upon different grounds and in a very different way. Within a few years past the steady stream of immigration has made European views and practices concerning this matter exceedingly familiar to us. The increased facilities of intercourse between nations have operated to bring us together, to show us one another's usages, and to put them in frequent and distinct contrast. The Lord's Day in New England — I instance New England as representative of what is best in the American churches — is a very different thing from the Lord's Day in Berlin, or even from the Lord's Day in Chicago, or even from the Lord's Day in New York and in Newark. In these last cities the American Sunday and the European Sunday are put side by side. We see the difference between them. We mark how each is modifying the other. We begin to fear lest the nation shall come to esteem every day alike; and not every day alike holy, but every day alike profane. And we shrink from the surrender of any voice of authority, of any force of law, which arrests or discourages such profanation. Already, we say, the tendency in what seems to us the wrong direction is strong enough and far too strong. Let us make our laws stricter. Let us hold more rigid theories than ever. Let us be more scrupulous in our observance than before. Let us denounce these foreign customs. Let us put upon them the stigma of our condemnation. Let us judge our brethren. Let us treat their customs with opprobrium and obloquy. Let us make them feel the strong restraint and penalty of civil law. At any rate, let us not, at such a time as this, give up the useful terrors of the Jewish commandment. Let us not weaken our case by untimely concessions. Let us even do a little evil, and defend our practice with a false sanction, in order that so great a good as the preservation of our Puritan Sabbath may come.

The temptation to do this is very strong and very plausible. But I do not think that the apostle Paul would have yielded to it. I do not think he would have given such advice as this. I think that he would say, as in the text he has said, "Let every man be fully persuaded in his own mind." There is a right way and a wrong way to deal with this case. The wrong way is to deal with it by force. The right way is to deal with it by conscience, respecting the liberty of conscience on the one hand, respecting the weakness of conscience on the other. I have very strong views on the question of comparison between the European Sabbath and the American Sabbath. I very greatly prefer our methods of employing and observing the day. I strongly deprecate the tendency to make of it a day of mere amusement, of animal enjoyment, of junketing and riot. But I would resist this tendency by fully persuading the minds of men that our way is the better way, and that it is demanded by the highest and most intelligent interpretation of the law of liberty, the law of love, the law of Christ. If I cannot do it thus, I do not want to do it at all.

Broadly stated, this is the difference between the European Sabbath and the American Sabbath. With us the day is a religious day exclusively. It is a day restricted to the uses of Christian worship and of Christian fellowship. Public amusements are discountenanced and forbidden. People are expected to spend their time at their own homes or in their places of worship, and in religious occupations. On the continent of Europe, and where European customs have been introduced among us, it is very different. People go to church in the morning, — that is to say, some of them do, not all of them, — but, after that, the day is given up to mere amusement. Great dinners are given. It is the day for public and official banquets. The avenues and parks are crowded with people walking and riding. It is the great day for military parades and public spectacles of every sort; for horse-races and things of that sort. In the evening all the places of amusement put forth their most attractive programmes, and are thronged with people. And of course, more or less generally, shops are open and workmen busy in supplying the wants of this great multitude of pleasure-seekers. It is a bright, merry, popular day, but not especially a devout or a religious day.

Between these two methods of observance I do not hesitate for a moment. Who that recalls the sacred stillness of a New England Sabbath, — from the moment when the church-bells fill the morning air with music, till the peace of evening settles down upon the deeper peace of holy fellowship with God, for which the day has given opportunity, — who that recalls the sanctity of the day as our fathers kept it, the resistless eloquence with which it spoke, even to the heedless and reluctant, of another world than this, a pure and holy world, a spiritual world, — the solemn sweetness with which it touched all souls, reminding them of one who died for all that all might live, of one who rose again that by the power of his resurrection we might be glorified, — who, I say, remembering this, will not say that our observance of the Lord's Day (or let us rather say our fathers' observance of the Lord's Day) as a spiritual day, was far better than the French observance of it, or the German observance of it, or the Roman observance of it as a day for sensuous and animal enjoyment? By as much as spirit is better than matter, by as much as soul is nobler than body, by as much as eternity is loftier than time, by so much is it better. So it seems to me.

Doubtless, our fathers' observance of the day was often overscrupulous, often legal and severe, often uncharitable even, in its intolerance. Doubtless it was defended by poor arguments; doubtless it was enforced with zeal which was not according to knowledge. But they were fully persuaded in their own minds, and they acted on their convictions with an heroic fidelity. They were spiritually-minded men, although sometimes severe in word and strict in deed. If we can improve upon the practice of our fathers in any particular, we are bound to do it. But it will be a good while before we improve upon the religiousness and devoutness of their spirit. So too, if in these respects we can learn any lessons, even from the Germans, whose observance of the day we on the whole disapprove, we are bound to do it. And if we can teach them any lessons, if we can show them any more excellent way, if we can share with them any inheritance of Christian method which is better than their own, as

I surely think we can, then we are bound to do that also.

And it seems to me (I say these things in the way of suggestion merely, and not at all in the spirit of authority), it seems to me that the same motives which impel us to the observance of the day at all, should impel us to the observance of it in a spiritual way, in a devout and religious way, in a Puritan way if you please to say so, rather than in the European way of secular amusement and animal recreation. What those motives were I need only remind you, since I dwelt at length upon them in the last discourse.

I said that love to Christ, whose resurrection from the dead this day celebrates, impels us to commemorate it. Because we love him, we love the day that reminds us of him. Because we love him, also, we shall so use the day that it shall best remind us of him. How shall it best remind us of him? By giving up its time to sport and merriment, by strollings in the streets, and gossipings in public places; by spectacles of worldly gayety, by noisy music, by sensuous eating and drinking, by theatres and concerts, by idleness and sloth? I think not, verily. By meditation on his truth, by communion with his saints, by worship in private and in public, by prayer for his Spirit, by praise for his redemption,— in such ways as these we shall be best reminded of him, in such ways as these we shall get nearest to him. And if opportunity is given us to speak of him to others, or to do in his name works of charity and brotherly kindness, in such ways we shall get still nearer to him, shall be in even sweeter fellowship with him. Gather your little ones about you, if God has given you little ones to train for him; gather them about you. Let the day become a very welcome day, a very happy day, to them; because, more than any other day, it is a household day, because the loving ties of natural affection find more full and beautiful expression than on other days. Let the thought of Christ be the deep undertone which charms and hallows all the day, and which is heard more full, more deep, more resonant with eternal music, in the Sunday stillness than when driving cares and roaring businesses and jarring discords of traffic, and passionate excitements of gain and loss, fill up the week. Take time to-day to think of Christ, to learn of Christ, to tell your little ones of Christ, to teach Christ to those who do not know him, to open the door of your house to Christ, and let him come and make your home a holy place, to open the door of your heart to Christ, and let him enter in and sup with you, and you with him.

Then, secondly, the way in which you keep this day must be determined by the love you bear your neighbor. Who is your neighbor? Well, for example, your man-servant and your maid-servant are your neighbors. The man who takes care of your horses is your neighbor. The woman who prepares your dinner is your neighbor. You are bound by the law of love to be considerate toward them, and to secure them in their enjoyment of their day of rest, and to give them the opportunity to think of Christ, to learn of Christ, to worship Christ. Because this day is a festival, we might properly enough celebrate some part of it with feasting and with "pious mirth," if it were not for this consideration. It was not that the day might be a fast-day that Moses commanded not to kindle fire nor to cook food upon the Sabbath: it was "that thy manservant and thy maidservant may rest as well as thou." So, too, it is not that the day is any way a sorrowful or gloomy day to us, that we content ourselves without festivities, which otherwise we might enjoy; but it is simply that our man-servant and maid-servant may have rest as well as we. It is not on the letter of the Jewish law that we ground any obligation of this sort. Indeed, we do not speak of it as obligation anyway, and have no right to lay down strict, unbending laws upon such matters. Circumstances alter cases. Something, for example, depends upon the willingness, upon the Christian liberty and love, even of our man-servant and our maid-servant, as to what service we may expect from them. And it is to the spirit of Christian liberty and love, and to that only, that we can make appeal. Only, "let every man be fully persuaded in his own mind."

Then, lastly, love to our own souls suggests what I have called the spiritual method of employing the Lord's Day, in preference to the simply sensuous way of using it. Bodily rest, indeed, we need. Let no man think that he can do without it. If he is forced by higher duties to deprive himself of it on Sunday, as a minister is, then he is bound to take it on Saturday or on Monday. And I may quote the fourth commandment as obliging me to observe Monday as a rest-day, with just as much emphasis, and no more than that with which you quote it for the observance of Sunday. Make this Lord's Day a day of rest to your bodies and your minds. Do not merely change your employments of the week for different but not less wearisome employments on this first day. The cases are exceptional which will justify you in doing so. Rest! It is a privilege, it is therefore a duty. It is especially a duty in this restless age and in this restless land. Do not think you are sinning if you sleep. You are sinning if you think so, but you need not think so. Refresh your body in such ways as seem to you best, considering as well the rights and the necessities of your neighbor as your own. Make the day a welcome day, a free day, a happy day, a day of privilege. Count it no sin to worship God through the enjoyment of his works in nature, beneath the temple of the groves, if so you choose, or among the lilies of the field, breathing his pure air, rejoicing in his blessed light, listening to the birds that sing his glory, and that sing because he works to give them life and tune their songs, — count this no sin, if it is needful to you, if it is helpful to you, if there are no higher duties to yourself or to your neighbors, which forbid it. But especially, and more than all, employ the day for spiritual rest, with thoughts of Christ, with meditation on the truth of Christ, with the communion of the saints of Christ, with worship in your home and in the church of Christ, "not forsaking the assembling of ourselves together, as the manner of some is; but exhorting one another; and so much the more as ye see the day approaching."

"So much the more as ye see the day approaching." What day? The day of the Lord. What day of the Lord? The day of his eternal Sabbath; the day of which this first day of the week is the perpetual promise and dawning; the day of God's rest; the day of the rest that remaineth for the people of God. For it is approaching. The first beams of it are gilding earth and heaven even now. It is not a day of hours and minutes. It is eternal. It is not a day that comes and goes. It "remaineth." It is not a day upon which there comes down the darkness of the night. "There is no night there." It is not a day upon which there comes in the turmoil and distraction, the temptation and the evil, of the week. "There shall in no wise enter into it any thing that defileth, neither whatsoever worketh abomination, or maketh a lie." This is the Sabbath day. This is the day which is approaching. It "cometh, and now is," in souls that love the Lord and know his peace and share his righteousness. And it shall shine more and more throughout eternal ages.

Into the likeness of this spiritual day should all our days be fashioned; for the blessedness of this eternal state should all our time be redeemed. If it were possible; but is it possible? For now, as when Paul wrote and labored, "the days are evil." Toil and trouble, traffic and speculation, the cares of this world, and the deceitfulness of riches, choke them and defile them. If, then, one day among the seven, as the weeks roll by, can be rescued from absorbing care and from deceitful business, and sanctified to the peculiar uses of religion and of charity, in God's name, and in the name of suffering and sinful men, let it be done. If there can be one day secured for rest and recreation to the weary sons of toil, one day for worship and religious thought and teaching, one day that shall prefigure and present by prophecy, and even by foretaste, the eternal blessedness of heaven, so let it be; and let it be this first day, the Lord's Day, full of golden memories and eloquent associations. Let it be kept as a perpetual privilege, an inalienable right, not with profane and noisy mirth, but with the sacred stillness of a joy and peace which the world cannot give nor take away. If there is given to us, by usage, by inheritance, by any sanction, such a day as this, we cannot afford to surrender it, we cannot afford to be remiss in our observance of it, or careless in our appreciation of its worth.

I have scarcely left myself a moment's space in which to speak of the relation of the civil law to the observance of the Lord's Day. But there is the less need for me to dwell upon this point, because the text itself, as I have now unfolded it, seems to indicate the true nature of that relation. If it be true that this observance is a matter for the individual conscience, then what the law has to do is to protect the rights of the individual conscience. It is bound to do no more than this, but it is bound to do this. If any man or any community is fully persuaded of the duty or the privilege of sanctifying any day to religious uses, they are to be protected in the performance of their duty and in the exercise of their privilege; their worship is to be defended from noise and disturbance; their rest is to be secured from the demands of business, so far as may be possible without infringement of the rights of others. Moreover, the State has an undoubted right, which, indeed, it continually exercises, to ordain by law certain days for the refreshment and recreation of its citizens, — on sanitary considerations, or for historical considerations, or for the sake of any wise expediency; and to require that on such days business of certain sorts shall be suspended; to close the governmental offices; to provide that contracts made on such days are not binding; to make of it what we call a legal holiday. It may do this every week, and in effect it does it when it sanctions the observance of the Lord's Day; and every government which is fully persuaded of the need of such a rest-day or holiday is even bound to ordain it. Only I would have you remember that government cannot make a day holy, that force cannot make a day holy. Acts of legislatures and of common councils may keep a day silent, may make it quiet; but they cannot keep it holy: and perhaps they will discover that they can keep it quiet only for a little while. Holiness is a thing of liberty, not a thing of force. If the observance of the Lord's Day is to be a holy observance, it must be a free observance. If men come to take Jesus "by force, to make him a king," he will withdraw himself alone. The service which is acceptable in his sight must be a reasonable service, a willing service. And, as I have said already, the glory of this

Christian festival above the Jewish festival is, notably, its freedom.

Now I have finished this discussion, and I desire only to recapitulate the argument with all possible conciseness.

1. First I tried to show, in the light of that venerable story in Genesis, interpreted by the commentary in the Epistle to the Hebrews, what the Sabbath is; affirming, that, in the highest and truest usage of the word, it is not a day of hours and minutes, but an eternal state, spiritual, heavenly; that it is the rest of God, and the rest which remaineth for the people of God.

We discovered also that there is a Sabbath work which God is doing, — the work of making holy the creation which he made good; and that, according as the people of God enter upon their rest (or Sabbatism), they also employ it in the same holy activity, in being good and doing good.

And we discovered also, that, though the real Sabbath is eternal in the heavens, there may be Sabbaths in some lower sense, — Sabbaths of days, Sabbaths made for man, shadows and types of the eternal rest in God for which man was made: and that, notably, there have been two such Sabbaths; the weekly Jewish Sabbath on the seventh day, and the weekly Christian Sabbath on the first day.

2. Then, secondly, we discussed the origin and history of the Jewish Sabbath, and inquired the meaning of it. We found that it was instituted in the wilderness as a monumental day; pointing forever backward to the slavery in Egypt and to the exodus from Egypt,—pointing forever forward, also, with "illusive" prophecy, to liberty and rest,—at first to Joshua and Canaan, then to David and the earthly kingdom, and then to the Son of David and the kingdom of heaven.

3. Then, thirdly, we discussed the use and indicated the abuse of the Jewish Sabbath: we found that it was meant to be a privilege, but was perverted to be an irksome bondage; that the Lord Jesus (as a Jew "made under the law") was the true exemplar of the right use of the institution, employing it lovingly, gratefully, gladly, as an ordinance "made for man;" and that the Pharisees in their disputes with Jesus

represented the abuse of the day, making it irksome and burdensome upon men, as if men were "made for" it.

4. Passing, then, to the Christian festival of the Lord's Day, I showed how it came to be observed, and, from the earliest ages of the Christian church, has always been observed, as a day of sacred privilege; I reminded you of the august significance of this first day of the week, — significance at once historic and prophetic; and I insisted, that not by the force of the Jewish commandment, but by the sanction of most venerable usage, by the dictate of manifest expediency, and so by the operation of the Christian law of love, it is to us a weekly Sabbath, to be welcomed and dearly cherished as an earnest of the real and perfect Sabbath.

5. Continuing the argument, I also pointed out the greater glory of the Christian Sabbath in comparison with the Jewish, as consisting, notably, in these three points: (1) that it is a free day, not resting upon commandments written and graven in stones, but on the voluntary and reasonable service of loving hearts; (2) that it is fast coming to be a universal day, and not

a day for one nation; and (3) that it is a more spiritual day, pointing, not through cloudy types and shadows, but directly, up to the spiritual and eternal rest, and to the risen Christ who gives it.

6. And now I have indicated what seems to me the proper method of observing this Lord's Day; warning against bondage on the one hand, and against license on the other.

So we cease the discussion where we began it, with the thought, the hope, the expectation, of the rest into which God is entered, and which remaineth for his people; and with the solemn undertone of blended encouragement and warning, which has sounded all the while, — Take heed, "a promise being left of entering into rest," that none of us "seem to come short of it."

www.ingramcontent.com/pod-product-compliance
Lightning Source LLC
Chambersburg PA
CBHW021346230426
43666CB00006B/424